Coping With Breast Cancer

✓ **Treatments** *That Work*™

Coping With Breast Cancer

A COUPLES-FOCUSED GROUP INTERVENTION

Therapist Guide

Sharon L. Manne • Jamie S. Ostroff

OXFORD
UNIVERSITY PRESS

2008

OXFORD
UNIVERSITY PRESS

Oxford University Press, Inc., publishes works that further
Oxford University's objective of excellence
in research, scholarship, and education.

Oxford   New York
Auckland   Cape Town   Dar es Salaam   Hong Kong   Karachi
Kuala Lumpur   Madrid   Melbourne   Mexico City   Nairobi
New Delhi   Shanghai   Taipei   Toronto

With offices in
Argentina   Austria   Brazil   Chile   Czech Republic   France   Greece
Guatemala   Hungary   Italy   Japan   Poland   Portugal   Singapore
South Korea   Switzerland   Thailand   Turkey   Ukraine   Vietnam

Published by Oxford University Press, Inc.
198 Madison Avenue, New York, New York 10016

www.oup.com

Oxford is a registered trademark of Oxford University Press

Library of Congress Cataloging-in-Publication Data

Manne, Sharon L.
    Coping with breast cancer : a couples-focused group intervention :
    therapist guide / Sharon L. Manne, Jamie S. Ostroff.
        p.   ;   cm. — (TreatmentsThatWork)
    Includes bibliographical references and index.
    ISBN 978-0-19-534290-1 (pbk. : alk. paper)
    1. Breast—Cancer—Psychological aspects.   2. Cognitive therapy.
    3. Marital psychotherapy.   I. Ostroff, Jamie S.   II. Title.   III. Series:
    Treatments that work.
    [DNLM: 1. Breast Neoplasms—psychology.   2. Cognitive
    Therapy—methods.   3. Couples Therapy—methods.   4. Interpersonal
    Relations.   5. Marital Therapy—methods. WP 870 M282c 2008]
    RC280.B8M337 2008
    616.99′44906—dc22
                                                        2007047488

ISBN-13 978-0-19-534290-1 Paper

1   3   5   7   9   8   6   4   2

Printed in the United States of America
on acid-free paper

About Treatments *ThatWork*™

Stunning developments in health care have taken place over the last several years, but many of our widely accepted interventions and strategies in mental health and behavioral medicine have been brought into question by research evidence as not only lacking benefit but, perhaps, inducing harm. Other strategies have been proven effective using the best current standards of evidence, resulting in broad-based recommendations to make these practices more available to the public. Several recent developments are behind this revolution. First, we have arrived at a much deeper understanding of pathology, both psychological and physical, which has led to the development of new, more precisely targeted interventions. Second, our research methodologies have improved substantially, such that we have reduced threats to internal and external validity, making the outcomes more directly applicable to clinical situations. Third, governments around the world and health care systems and policymakers have decided that the quality of care should improve, that it should be evidence based, and that it is in the public's interest to ensure that this happens (Barlow, 2004; Institute of Medicine, 2001).

Of course, the major stumbling block for clinicians everywhere is the accessibility of newly developed evidence-based psychological interventions. Workshops and books can go only so far in acquainting responsible and conscientious practitioners with the latest behavioral health care practices and their applicability to individual patients. This new series, Treatments*ThatWork*™, is devoted to communicating these exciting new interventions to clinicians on the front lines of practice.

The manuals and workbooks in this series contain step-by-step detailed procedures for assessing and treating specific problems and diagnoses. But this series also goes beyond the books and manuals by providing ancillary materials that will approximate the supervisory process in assisting practitioners in the implementation of these procedures in their practice.

In our emerging health care system, the growing consensus is that evidence-based practice offers the most responsible course of action for the mental health professional. All behavioral health care clinicians deeply desire to provide the best possible care for their patients. In this series, our aim is to close the dissemination and information gap and make that possible.

This therapist guide and the companion workbook for couples outline a group therapy program for couples dealing with a breast cancer diagnosis. One in eight women will be diagnosed with breast cancer during their lifetime. As women undergo treatment for their cancer, their partners have an important role to play in providing emotional support. Many couples dealing with breast cancer can benefit from intervention to help them cope as a unit.

This couples-focused group program is for women diagnosed with early stage breast cancer and their partners. It has been proven to reduce psychological distress and improve well-being in cancer patients. The aim is to improve a couple's functioning as a "team" as they face the challenges of coping with cancer. Couples learn effective support, communication, intimacy-enhancing, and stress-management skills. The group format helps with skill acquisition through modeling and provides a supportive environment for couples. This guide makes an important contribution to improving quality of life through improving a couple's relationship.

David H. Barlow, Editor-in-Chief,
Treatments*ThatWork*™
Boston, MA

References

Barlow, D. H. (2004). Psychological treatments. *American Psychologist, 59,* 869–878.

Institute of Medicine. (2001). *Crossing the quality chasm: A new health system for the 21st century.* Washington, DC: National Academy Press.

Contents

Acknowledgments

The authors would like to dedicate this book to the women diagnosed with breast cancer and their partners who have participated in their research for the past 15 years. They would also like to thank the National Institutes of Health for their support of this research (R01 CA 77857, R01 CA 78084, and K05 CA 109332).

Chapter 1 *Introductory Information for Therapists*

Background Information and Purpose of This Program

The purpose of this couples-focused program is to reduce psychological distress and enhance well-being of women diagnosed with early stage breast cancer and their partners. We achieve this improved quality of life by focusing on the dyad and more specifically on the quality and functioning of their relationship. Our goal is to enhance couples' ability to provide effective support to one another, assist them in communicating more effectively about the challenges and stresses they have undergone and will undergo related to breast cancer, and enhance couples' ability to cope with cancer as a cohesive "team" rather than as two individuals. Therefore, what distinguishes this approach from other psychological interventions for individuals with early stage breast cancer is the focus on the couple as a unit rather than on the individual patient or caregiver.

The couple-focused group intervention is guided by cognitive-social processing theory and cognitive-behavioral and behavioral theories, as well as empirical findings supporting these theories. Cognitive-social processing theory suggests that people adjust successfully to difficult life experiences by trying either to assimilate (e.g., do not change one's view) or to accommodate (e.g., change) the experience into their view of the world (e.g., fairness) or of themselves (e.g., mortality). Most people do not work on adapting to difficult life events such as the diagnosis as cancer alone—rather, they talk about their thoughts and feelings with family and friends to obtain emotional support and advice. Sharing thoughts and feelings with close others may assist in learning to tolerate upsetting feelings, facilitating finding meaning and benefit in the experience, and helping to assimilate and accommodate the cancer experience. Conversely, not being able to comfortably share one's feelings and thoughts about

1

a difficult life experience because the person feels one's family and/or friends may not be interested or supportive can interfere with one's ability to successfully adapt to the experience. Research suggests that women diagnosed with early stage breast cancer are likely to consider their partner as the primary source for emotional support during the cancer experience (Pistrang & Barker, 1992; 1995). Similarly, partners of women diagnosed with breast cancer are likely to nominate the ill partner as a primary confidante during the cancer experience (Northouse et al., 2001). Therefore, any barriers to open sharing of reactions to the breast cancer experience and the reciprocal provision of satisfactory support between partners may interfere with couples' effectively coping with this experience. Our previous research suggested that partners' supportive and unsupportive responses were associated with patient distress (Manne et al., 1997), and that lower levels of open communication between partners were associated with greater distress on the part of women diagnosed with cancer (Manne et al., 1999). Our results suggested that spouses' unsupportive responses predicted more limited coping responses (avoidance coping), which in turn were predictive of greater negative affect (Manne et al., 1999). Spouses' support predicted more positive coping and had a direct effect on higher positive affect and lower negative affect (Manne et al., 1999).

Based on theory and empirical research, the couple-focused group intervention seeks to promote open communication, as well as supportive interactions between partners. This goal is achieved by teaching couples to enhance their ability to communicate effectively with and provide satisfactory support to one another. The group process also facilitates the social sharing of emotional reactions in a supportive environment.

As mentioned, the intervention was also guided by cognitive-behavior and behavioral principals. Cognitive-behavior theory proposes that emotional reactions are largely determined by one's interpretation of experiences such as one's thoughts and underlying assumptions and beliefs. Behavioral theory proposes that reactions to most situations are learned, and that these responses can be changed. Interventions based on both theories are skill based. These approaches typically teach individuals new ways of responding to stressful experiences. Modeling and practice are key intervention strategies. Cognitive-behavioral and behavioral treatments are incorporated into the couple-focused group treatment as both in-session and home assignment exercises. The goals of these intervention techniques fall into four categories:

1. Improving communication and support skills

   - Identifying and adopting good communication strategies
   - Learning and abstaining from destructive communication strategies
   - Identifying what the other partner considers supportive

2. Improving stress management skills: learning different ways of relaxing as a couple

3. Improving sexual intimacy: enhancing skills

   - Sensate focus
   - Learning about the impact of breast cancer on sexual intimacy

4. Improving the couple's ability to evaluate the impact of cancer on the couple and set relationship goals

   - Identifying new relationship priorities and goals
   - Developing a post–cancer treatment relationship identity

Disorder or Problem Focus

This intervention focuses on women undergoing treatment for early stage breast cancer and their partners. We do not target a psychological or psychiatric disorder but rather normative psychosocial reactions to a very difficult life stressor. However, it is possible that either patient or partner interested in this program will evidence either a prior psychiatric history or recent onset of significant anxiety or depressive symptoms in response to the diagnosis of breast cancer. As noted in the chapter on group logistics, we recommend that the leader meet with each couple prior to the onset of the group to evaluate the level of marital distress, presence of a serious psychiatric disorder (e.g., thought disorder), or substance use. If the couple is maritally distressed and/or substance abuse or serious psychiatric disorder is an issue for either partner, we do not recommend the couple be included in the group. Instead, we recommend referral of these couples to more intensive individual or marital treatment.

The couple-focused group intervention was developed by Drs. Manne and Ostroff based on long-standing research in the area. Session content was guided by the main goals of this intervention. Key features of the intervention strategies selected were (a) the intervention content was couple focused and encouraged a relationship perspective on cancer's effects; (b) the intervention content facilitated effective communication between partners; and (c) the intervention could be delivered in a group format. Content drawn from other treatments was adapted specifically for the cancer and couples' group context.

The "fishbowl" exercise in Session 1 and the relationship priorities and goal-setting exercises in Session 6 were adapted from Steinglass and colleagues' Multiple Family Discussion Group (Gonzales, Steinglass, & Reiss, 1989; Ostroff, Steinglass, Ross et al., 2004). Communication skill content was based on the Prevention and Relationship Enhancement Program (Markman & Floyd, 1980) and on the work of Gottman and colleagues (Gottman, Notarius, Gonso, & Markman, 1976). Sample content from these sources includes the Speaker/Listener Technique, effective and ineffective communication skills, the Intimacy Deck, and Caring Days activity. Support skills content was based on the authors' previous research on the relationship between spouse supportive and unsupportive responses and patient adaptation to cancer (e.g., Manne et al., 1997, 1999). Stress management content was based on Lazarus and Folkman's Stress and Coping Theory (Lazarus and Folkman, 1984) and supporting research on effective and ineffective methods of coping with stressors such as cancer (e.g., Carver et al., 1993; Manne et al., 1999). Relaxation techniques were drawn from Jacobson (1974) and others (e.g., Davis et al., 1982). Sensate focus exercises were based on Masters and Johnson (1966) and others (Kaplan, 1974), and thought restructuring skill content were based on Beck and colleagues (1979). Illustrations of communication skills were taken directly from the authors' previous research on couples' interactions and adjustment to breast cancer (Manne et al., 2004). Content regarding resuming sexual activity and survivorship issues was drawn from the authors' clinical experience working with couples coping with sexual sequelae of cancer treatment.

A pilot testing of the couple-focused intervention was conducted with a group of four couples in the winter of 1996. Couples participated in six 90-minute group sessions, which had the following topics: Introduction/Coping Skills, Impact of Cancer on the Marital Relationship, Communication, and Maintaining Sexual Intimacy (Manne & Ostroff, unpublished data). Content was similar to the content of the final couple-focused group intervention. The authors tried different in-group exercises to determine their feasibility and acceptability. Feedback was solicited from group members, and their feedback was incorporated into the treatment.

This information led to the development of a two-phase, 5-year grant proposal submitted to and subsequently funded by the National Institutes of Health in 1998. The first phase of the research grant, which was conducted between 1998 and 2000, involved a two-part study that included videotaped observation of couples discussing cancer-related and general marital issues and a paper-and-pencil longitudinal study. The results of the coding of the observed couples' interactions indicated that women diagnosed with early stage breast cancer reported lower psychological distress when their partners responded to their self-disclosures about cancer-related concerns by offering reciprocal self-disclosure as well as support-related communication (Manne et al., 2005). Results from the paper-and-pencil longitudinal study indicated that partner critical responses lead to increases in patient distress (Manne et al., 2005), that mutual constructive communication lead to reduced distress among both patients and partners and mutual avoidance of discussing concerns lead to increased distress among both patients and partners (Manne et al., 2006), and that efforts to conceal worries and concerns on the part of either partner were associated with increases in both patient and partner distress (Manne et al., 2007).

After initial analyses of the results from the first phase, the authors began the second phase of the research, which was the randomized clinical trial evaluating the efficacy of the couple-focused group intervention. The intervention program content was refined based upon the results of a longitudinal study in the following ways: (a) Exercises in which partners practiced meeting one another's support needs were added; (b) videotaped segments were developed to illustrate effective and ineffective communication skills based on videotaped segments from the observational study; (c) additional relaxation skills and practice exercises were added; (d) in-session "playful" exercises to illustrate key points and facilitate rapport and support between group members were added (these included the getting to know each other exercise in Session 1 and the "Not-So-Newlywed Game" in Session 2); (e) additional content on sexuality was added in the form of videotaped segments from a publicly available tape illustrating common sexual and intimacy issues couples face during breast cancer; and (f) the Sensate Focus exercise was added to Session 3.

Once the treatment manual was finalized, the randomized trial was conducted with patients recruited from either the Fox Chase Cancer Center, Memorial Sloan-Kettering Cancer Center, or several other participating hospitals. The major results of this trial were published in the *Journal of Consulting and Clinical Psychology* (2005). Two hundred thirty-eight women who had been diagnosed and treated for early stage breast cancer and their partners were randomly assigned to either the couple-focused group intervention condition or the usual care condition. Usual care consisted of the standard psychosocial care that was available to all participants at each of the study sites. Of the 120 couples assigned to the six-session, couple-focused group intervention, 42 couples did not attend any group sessions and 78 couples attended between one and six sessions. Participants completed follow-up surveys that were administered at 1 week and 6 months postintervention. All patients, even those who dropped out of the couple-focused group, were asked to complete follow-up surveys assessing mood, functional impairment, and partner unsupportive behavior. Data were analyzed using growth curve modeling and intent-to-treat analyses. Moderating effects for preintervention levels of physical impairment and perceived unsupportive partner behavior were evaluated. Treatment fidelity was rated on a random selection of 44% of session videotapes, and group facilitators' fidelity to the treatment manual was excellent.

Results indicated that the couple-focused group intervention resulted in a significant reduction in patients' depressive symptoms. Tests for the moderating effects of preintervention perceptions of unsupportive partner behavior indicated that, among women who rated their partners as more unsupportive, those assigned to the couple-focused group intervention reported less distress and greater well-being at follow up than did women in the usual care group. There were marginally lower cancer-specific distress scores among women reporting more physical impairment preintervention in the couple-focused group intervention compared with women in the usual care condition. Subgroup analyses that examined whether women who attended group sessions differed from women who were assigned to the group sessions but did not attend them indicated that women who attended the intervention reported significantly greater reductions in distress and improvements in well-being compared with women who were assigned to attend the group but did not attend sessions. Moderating effects for preintervention perceptions of unsupportive partner behavior and physical impairment were present.

Follow-up analyses of cognitive-social moderators of the couple-focused group intervention (Manne et al., 2007) indicated that the couple-focused group intervention was more effective for women who began the group sessions reporting higher levels of emotional expression (i.e., expressing their feelings about cancer as a way of coping) and emotional processing (i.e., attempts to delve into one's emotional reactions to cancer).

What Is CBT?

This treatment is based primarily on principles of cognitive-behavioral therapy. The treatment focuses on learning communication skills, support skills, intimacy-enhancing skills, and stress management skills and adaptive methods of coping with cancer more effectively as a dyad or team. Couples are encouraged to examine changes in their perspectives and views about the relationship and their priorities in their relationship as a result of breast cancer and consider long-term changes they wish to make in the relationship.

CBT Model of Couple-Focused Group Intervention

The therapy techniques used in this intervention are largely based on principles of cognitive-behavioral and behavioral therapy in that the focus is on skills acquisition. It is proposed that the primary mechanisms that are responsible for therapeutic change are improvements in the ability to provide effective marital support, improved stress management skill, and the ability to find benefit and meaning in the cancer experience. In addition, modeling of effective communication and coping skills by other members of the group, by the group leaders, and by other couples as seen in the videotaped segments that group members observe is also likely responsible for skill acquisition.

It should also be noted that, because this is a group therapy approach, it is likely that nonspecific aspects of therapy are also responsible for therapeutic changes in addition to cognitive-behavioral mechanisms. Nonspecific mechanisms include the bond with the other members of the group as well as the group leaders and the support provided by group members and the leaders.

To date, there is no empirical evidence to support any putative mechanisms of change for this intervention.

Risks and Benefits of This Treatment Program

The main risk associated with this treatment approach is inherent in any group psychotherapy intervention. Some individuals may find it stressful to discuss difficult life events, and some individuals may find it difficult to share private feelings in front of others. In addition, some couples may find it difficult to discuss their sexual experiences in front of others. Social comparisons are an inevitable reaction to any group process, and group therapists can reduce the likelihood of negative social comparisons ("We're not doing as well as the Joneses") by normalizing the natural variation in relationships, as well as the unique strengths of all participating couples.

Benefits of this program include reductions in psychological distress and improvements in well-being as reported by women diagnosed with breast cancer (Manne et al., 2005). We do not have data regarding the impact on partners' distress and well-being. The randomized clinical trial evaluating this intervention indicated that the couple-focused group intervention resulted in the greatest reductions in distress among women who reported that their partners engaged in a greater-than-average frequency of unsupportive responses to their cancer compared with women reporting below-average unsupportive responses on the part of their partners who were in the couple-focused group intervention and compared with women who were assigned to usual care (Manne et al., 2005). The results of this study also indicated that women who began the group sessions with higher levels of physical impairment may benefit more from the group intervention (Manne et al., 2005).

Alternative Treatments

Three alternative published treatments have included partners in interventions for women diagnosed with breast cancer. Nezu and colleagues (2003) examined the efficacy of a problem-solving therapy among breast cancer patients and their partners. Depressed cancer patients received either 10 sessions of individual problem-solving skills therapy, 10 sessions of problem-solving skills therapy with a significant other present for support and guidance, or a wait-list control. At posttreatment, all participants who received problem-solving therapy reported less distress than wait-list control patients. No differences in distress were identified between the individual and partner-assisted problem-solving therapy. At a 6-month follow-up, however, patients who received problem-solving along with their significant other reported lower levels of psychological distress than did patients who received individual problem-solving therapy on several distress outcome measures. These effects were further maintained 1-year posttreatment.

Scott and colleagues (2004) conducted a randomized clinical trial evaluating the efficacy of a couples-based coping training for women with either breast or gynecologic cancers. Ninety-four married women with early stage cancer and their partners were randomly assigned to couples-based coping training (CanCOPE), individual coping training for the woman, or a medical education control. CanCOPE reduced psychological distress among the female participants compared with the individual coping training and medical education control.

Kalaitzi and colleagues (2007) have recently developed and evaluated a 6-session structured combination of brief couples and sex therapy. Sessions focus on desensitization to the mastectomy scar and resuming sexual contact. The study of 40 women with in situ breast cancer and mastectomy and their partners indicated that CBPI patients showed significant improvement in depression and state anxiety scores, as well as in body image, satisfaction with relationship, presumed attractiveness to their partner, orgasm frequency, and communicating their desire.

The Role of Medications

Because this program is focused on psychological and relationship reactions to a medical problem, psychotropic medication is not formally recommended. However, we recommend that group leaders informally monitor participants during the group, and if the group leaders observe signs of significant distress we recommend that they meet separately with the participant(s) after the group session to evaluate distress formally. We recommend that participants who report clinically significant depression and/or anxiety be referred to psychiatric and psychological resources available in your clinical or community setting.

Outline of This Treatment Program

Session 1

1. Introductions and brief description of first group meeting

2. Program overview, including goals, objectives, group rules, and session format; discussion of homework assignments

3. Icebreaker activity: getting to know you exercise

4. Fishbowl exercise: a subgroup of the cancer patients "meet" with one of the cotherapists to discuss the patient perspective on cancer and its effect on marital life; partners observe this discussion

5. Partners who had been observing reflect, led by the other coleader, the patient subgroup discussion

6. A subgroup of the partners "meet" with one of the cotherapists to discuss the partner perspective on cancer and its effect on marital life; patients observe this discussion.

7. Patients who had been observing reflect, led by the other coleader, the partner subgroup discussion

8. Feedback from participants on the first meeting; focus on couples' expectations in joining the group, questions that have arisen as a result of the first meeting, and what participants' goals are for the group

9. Review schedule of meetings and make any necessary changes to ensure attendance of all couples at all meetings; provide administrative information

Session 2

1. Review of previous session

2. Present material on stress; allow participants to contribute to lecture by making a list (on a flipchart or white board) of illness-related stressors and stress responses

3. Group activity: Reading the Signs of Stress exercise and the "Not-So-Newlywed Game"

4. Introduce relaxation techniques and lead group in Focused Breathing exercise

5. Home assignments: (a) have couples review the Reading the Signs of Stress worksheet and discuss at home using discussion questions provided in the workbook; (b) practice Focused Breathing relaxation technique

Session 3

1. Review home assignments: Reading the Signs of Stress exercise and Focused Breathing relaxation technique

2. Discuss the impact of cancer on sexuality

3. Introduce material on physical affection and sexuality

4. Have couples create an Intimacy Deck in session

5. Describe Sensate Focus

6. Conduct Progressive Muscle Relaxation exercise in group

7. Home assignments: (a) select an activity from the Intimacy Deck to complete between sessions; (b) Sensate Focus exercise; (c) Progressive Muscle Relaxation

Session 4

1. Review home assignments: Intimacy Deck, Sensate Focus, and Progressive Muscle Relaxation

2. Lead interactive discussion on destructive communication patterns, common courtesies for effective communication, and expressing criticism (the X-Y-Z Technique); encourage participants to generate ideas and record ideas on flipchart or white board; engage couples in communication role-plays based on transcripts of conversations between breast cancer patients and their spouses

3. Introduce Speaker/Listener Technique and have couples practice the technique

4. Introduce first home assignment: instruct couples to use Speaker/Listener Technique to discuss a specific problem they are experiencing during or following cancer treatment

5. Conduct Guided Imagery Relaxation exercise with the group.

6. Home assignments: (a) Practice using the Speaker/Listener Technique; (b) Guided Imagery Relaxation

Session 5

1. Review home assignments: Speaker/Listener Technique, X-Y-Z Technique, and Guided Imagery Relaxation

2. Review communication/support material, eliciting group discussion

3. Group members practice expressing and listening to support needs with their partner

4. Members discuss support needs as a group and share reactions to partner's needs

5. Introduce Caring Days exercise

6. Couples generate and discuss Caring Days wish lists

7. Home assignment: Caring Days

Session 6

1. Review home assignment: Caring Days

2. Outline of psychosocial challenges of cancer survivorship and expectations for continued recovery

3. Couples construct Priority Pie Charts for before and after cancer

4. Couple-specific discussion of ways of coping with future demands of cancer, leading to the nomination of a "motto" for living with cancer

5. Presentation of pies and mottoes to the rest of the group with interview by group leaders

6. Wrap-up discussion

Use of the Workbook

The workbook contains summaries of each session for review and reinforcement, as well as handouts that participants can use for the in-session exercises. The workbook also contains home assignments and exercises to be done between sessions. Forms that participants complete for particular home exercises are also included. There are enough copies of relevant forms and worksheets that each couple can share a workbook.

It is recommended that couples bring their workbooks to each session. We also recommend that participants use the workbook during the session.

Chapter 2 *Group Logistics*

Forming a Group

Recruitment of Couples

Eligible participants for this group are women who (a) are diagnosed with early stage (ductal carcinoma in situ, Stage 1 to 2B) breast cancer who are in active treatment for this disease (active treatment is defined as being within 6 months of breast cancer diagnosis); (b) are currently married or in a committed relationship; (c) have a partner of either gender (lesbian couples have participated in this group); (d) are English speaking; and (e) are free of other serious psychiatric and active substance abuse conditions. We do not recommend this program for couples who are seriously considering separation or divorce.

With regard to group cohesion, we have found that it is particularly helpful to have a wide variation in age, ethnicity, marital duration, and family status (children in the home or not). We have found that diversity adds to the richness of the group.

Recruitment Procedures

We suggest the following options for group recruitment: (a) clinic announcements and advertisements, Web-based hospital announcements, waiting room pamphlets and posters; (b) referrals from oncologists, nurses, psychologists and psychiatrists, and social workers; (c) supplementing patients who are in individual or couples counseling in your practice.

Screening Group Members

We strongly recommend that group leaders meet with prospective couples to review expectations for involvement, confirm commitment for attendance, and answer preenrollment questions. In addition, we recommend that the group leaders interview couples to screen for serious psychiatric conditions, substance abuse, and severe marital conflict (seriously considering separation or divorce). These couples should be referred for further counseling (e.g., marital counseling, substance abuse treatment).

Group Size

Although we recommend two group facilitators, we recognize that this will not be feasible in all clinical settings. If the group leader is familiar with group content and has conducted previous couples' groups, we have found that the group can be successfully implemented by one facilitator.

The ideal group size ranges from four to six couples. If a group has fewer than four couples, we have found that there is less interaction, and a greater pressure on the attendees to disclose. In addition, if a couple does not attend a session due to medical or other reasons, it is difficult for the group to proceed comfortably. We do not recommend groups larger than six couples because of time constraints. If there are more than six couples, each one may not have the chance to participate in group discussions. Also, it is harder to maintain control over larger groups.

If the group consists of four couples, we recommend that you consider adjusting the time allotments for group activities. For example, you might consider shortening the length of in-session exercises or shortening the group duration. It is important to note that this is a closed group, and we do not recommend adding couples to the groups after the sessions have begun.

In-session exercises do require couples to break off into dyads or groups of two at times. We suggest that the group leaders have members sit around a large table. It is possible to conduct this group with members sitting in a circle if there are tables available for some of the in-session exercises. We do not suggest this group be conducted in a classroom setting or large auditorium because the chairs need to move, and desks do not facilitate group interaction.

Group Meetings and Program Duration

This program is composed of six, 90-minute sessions. We recommend that sessions be held on a weekly basis. However, because some women participating in the program may be actively involved in medical treatment at the time, flexibility in scheduling may be needed. In addition, we recommend that the group leaders discuss the calendar of planned group dates during the initial interview session with each couple. If this cannot be done, then a discussion of this topic should be planned for the first session. We have found that this discussion facilitates commitment and attendance. We have also found that rescheduling groups with a 1-week hiatus did not interfere with the implementation of the groups. Couples can record the program schedule in the space provided in their workbooks for quick and easy reference.

Maintenance or Follow-Up Sessions

This program does not include maintenance or follow-up sessions. Couples who request a follow-up session should be referred to local support groups or individual couples' therapy with a licensed marriage and family therapist (MFT) or other mental health professional.

Procedures Specific to This Group

Specialized Tools

We recommend that group leaders prepare a toolbox that contains the following materials to be used at every session:

- A copy of the workbook for reference, which contains all handouts and worksheets that couples will need throughout the program (see Chapter 1 for more information)

- Pens/pencils for couples to use during in-session exercises

- A flipchart or dry erase board on which group leaders can write session agendas, and important themes and concepts

  We also suggest that you have healthful snacks on hand for group members, particularly because most groups will be conducted in the early evening hours. We have found that it may be helpful to elicit input from participants regarding the types of snacks they would like.

  In addition to the toolbox materials listed, you will be required to provide and/or create the following additional resources for use in Session 3:

- Copies of the American Cancer Society (ACS) brochure "Sexuality & Cancer: For the Woman Who Has Cancer and Her Partner." Brochures can be obtained free of charge through the American Cancer Society by calling 1-800-ACS-2345.

- Sensate Focus cards: You will need to create these cards prior to Session 3 because they will be distributed to couples in session during the Intimacy Deck activity. You may use 3-by-5 index cards and the template provided at the end of Chapter 5 to create the sensate cards. Alternatively, you may download the template from the Treatments*ThatWork*™ Web site at www.oup.com/us/ttw.

Special Issues

A major issue that comes up in these groups is the amount of discussion about medical topics with medical terminology and interactions with medical staff. While we understand that this is an important issue for couples, we have found that unmonitored and unchecked discussion of the doctors or latest medical treatments, or complaints about medical problems, interferes with the designated focus of this group on how couples cope with cancer. In the first session, there is time set aside for couples to talk about their cancer story. While a discussion of medical issues is important at this time, group leaders should make a point of shifting the focus of the discussion to the impact of the medical issues on the couple and their relationship.

Another issue that may arise is the experiencing of an acute medical event by one of the couples in group. If this occurs, group leaders may check in with the couple, but we recommend doing so only after the group has been completed. Leaders can provide the patient and partner with support and refer the patient to her treating health professionals.

Group Rules

Group rules are as follows:

- Keep it confidential

- Show up to all meetings on time

- Call ahead if unable to attend a meeting

- Do not interrupt other group members when they are speaking

- Contact outside of sessions and the exchange of phone numbers and contact information are neither encouraged nor discouraged

- Do the homework

- Participate fully during the group (e.g., do the in-session exercises)

- One partner can participate in a session if the other partner cannot make it

Troubleshooting

We have found that several issues are typical of this particular group program. The following sections briefly discuss each one and the actions group leaders can take.

Nonattendance

With regard to nonattendance, we recommend that leaders do the following:

- Emphasize that maximum benefit will be achieved by attending each group.

- Encourage couples to commit as much as possible to the group sessions.

- Recognize the physical and emotional demands of undergoing cancer treatment and normalize nonattendance for medical reasons.

It is important to recognize that cancer treatment is a very stressful experience, and it is normal that patients and their partners may have difficulty meeting all responsibilities. This more liberal attendance policy underscores the benefit of recruiting five to six couples rather than three or four.

Dropouts

We have found that it is important to handle dropouts, particularly after Session 1, by recognizing this fact and discussing it briefly at the beginning of the group meeting. We suggest that the group leaders address couples who drop out by reframing this as a reflection of the difficulty of managing the cancer treatment process and all its demands, as well as a reflection of the couples' readiness to deal with relationship issues during a serious medical crisis. We have allowed participants who are present to discuss their reactions to the loss briefly at the beginning of the group, particularly if a couple drops out in the later sessions.

Death

Because of the short-term nature of this group and enrollment of patients in the early stages of breast cancer, the likelihood of death in this group is low. However, we recognize the uncertainty of cancer and its treatment and that it is possible for a group member to either become very ill or die. We recommend that the group leaders consider it the patient's responsibility to share whatever information they wish to disclose to the other group members.

The Disruptive Couple

If there is a disruptive couple in group (a couple who argues with one another), we suggest that the group leader adopt a structured stance when they engage in an argument during a session. The types of interventions we recommend are acknowledging that the issue the couple is arguing about is important to them, but then emphasizing the necessity of moving on with the program. If the couple continues to have in-session conflicts, we suggest that the group leader speak directly to them after the session and discuss possible options (e.g., referral to couples' counseling).

The Perfect Couple

Sometimes there are couples who present as having a "perfect" marriage (adopting a superior stance), and this can cause problems in the group. With regard to the "perfect couple," we suggest that the group leader reinforce that every couple has strengths and weaknesses. If group leaders perceive that other participants are put off or intimidated by the perfect couple, they should redirect the group discussion by stating that it is important to give other couples a chance to share their experiences. Within this skill-based approach, it is not part of the content of the groups to challenge or interpret this stance. However, we advocate taking an active stance to redirect attention away from the couple as appropriately as possible.

Not Completing Homework

Group participation will involve assignments to be completed at home between sessions. It is important to reinforce in the first session the importance of engaging in these assignments. Completion of homework is essential to benefiting from participation. However, if participants do not complete homework, group leaders should allow them to take the last turn in the sharing of their experience with the assignment, reinforce the importance of completing at-home assignments in a nonconfrontive manner, and then ask the participants to try again.

Role of Group Leaders

The role of group leaders is (a) to remain as close to the structured content of the group as possible (time allotments) and discuss group leader roles; (b) to provide information and structure to the group; (c) to offer observations about group members and processes; (d) to provide support to group members.

It is important that the group leaders recognize that this is not an insight-oriented process group. Interpretations with regard to couples' processes and historical interpretations are not considered appropriate for this cognitive-behavioral approach., While group process and support are important, group leaders need to recognize that group cohesion is very high with this type of structured group. It is not necessary to allow for a great deal of extended personal disclosures or off-topic discussion.

Group leaders should adopt an informal collaborative relationship and stance with one another. We believe that this serves as a model of the type of collaboration that we hope to achieve both between couples and between group members. We strongly encourage group leaders to model open communication and problem solving for members.

The group manual provides time allotments for each topic. We strongly recommend that one group leader serve as the "timekeeper," and that leaders make every attempt to be timely. Otherwise, important content may not be addressed, and then the group is not as effective. Group leaders should remind members who the timekeeper is to reduce the disruption of having a leader remind the group to move on. In addition, we suggest that the leaders discuss in advance who will be covering what topic, as well as what role they will take in the in-session content.

Training Group Leaders

We recommend that group leaders have a master's-level degree or higher (doctoral degree) in counseling, clinical psychology, or social work and have previous experience leading groups, couples, and medically ill patients and their families. One advantage of having two leaders per group is that it allows for a balancing of previous experience levels and strengths.

We have found it helpful to train new group leaders by pairing the new leader with a more experienced leader who has conducted previous groups using this manual. This provides for excellent on-site modeling and training.

Treatment fidelity can be enhanced by the use of the fidelity checklists provided in Appendix B. The fidelity checklists can be used for supervision. It is also possible to conduct supervision, particularly with regard to how to deal with difficult issues.

If it is considered helpful and feasible in your setting, videotaping group meetings allows for the most intense review and processing of sessions by group leaders.

We recommend that group leaders have a short debriefing session at the conclusion of each group session, during which they troubleshoot difficult couples and issues that arose in the group and make a plan for managing these issues.

We have attempted to include sufficient information in this manual and the corresponding workbook for leaders to effectively lead groups with the materials provided. However, if desired, the authors of this treatment are available for training and consultation sessions.

Chapter 3 · *Session 1*

(Corresponds to chapter 1 of the workbook)

Materials Needed

- Flipchart and markers
- Name tags
- Pens/pencils and paper

Session Outline

- Introduce yourself and your coleader and describe format of the first session (5 minutes)
- Provide overview of the program (5 minutes)
- Conduct icebreaker: getting to know you exercise (20 minutes)
- Have one group leader meet with a small subgroup of patients to discuss patient perspective on cancer and its effect on marital life while partners observe (15 minutes)
- Partners, led by group coleader, reflect on patient subgroup discussion (10 minutes)
- Have one group leader meet with small subgroup of partners to discuss the partner perspective on cancer and its effect on marital life while patients observe (15 minutes)
- Patients, led by group coleader, reflect on partner subgroup discussion (10 minutes)

- Review schedule of meetings and administrative information
  (5 minutes)

Session Objectives

- To orient participants to the group

- To foster connections among participants

- To facilitate expression of feelings and listening skills

Introductions (5 minutes)

Group leaders are advised to arrive in the meeting room several minutes before the appointed starting time to talk informally with arriving participants (the drive to class, the weather, etc.) while awaiting the arrival of other group members. The use of first names is suggested.

To begin the first meeting, introduce yourself and your coleader and welcome the couples to the group. Each group leader should describe his or her cancer-related expertise and his or her professional experience working with couples and groups.

Describe the format of the first meeting: (a) couples will participate in an activity to get to know each other, (b) an overview of the program will be given, (c) the group will begin exploration of the impact of cancer on the marital relationships, (d) feedback will be requested about the first meeting, (e) administrative details will be handled.

Program Overview (5 minutes)

The description of the program by one of the group leaders is an important part of the educational component of the group. These remarks should include the following points:

Recently, there has been a great deal of interest in how breast cancer patients and their partners cope with their illness and treatment.

While it appears that many patients adjust quite well, there are nonetheless issues and concerns that are shared by many patients, as well as their partners. Among those concerns are: how to deal with the side effects of treatment, concerns about the reactions of children, other family members, and friends; worries about the illness, treatment, or the future; and sadness. These concerns can interfere with the psychological adjustment of the patient and her partner. When couples work together to manage these concerns and are able to talk to each other, couples cope better with many of these side effects.

In studies examining the effects of breast cancer, a number of factors have been shown to be predictive of lower distress of patients and their partners. Good communication with one's partner figures prominently in these factors. Effective communication with one's partner about feelings and issues of concern, expression of support needs, and effective conveying of support have been related to lower levels of distress in patients and their partners. Good communication is good for relationships in general.

Other research has shown that effective coping skills are also important in adjusting to breast cancer diagnosis and treatment. Productive coping strategies, constructive problem solving, and appraisal of stressful situations are among the coping behaviors that appear to lead to lower levels of distress and help patients and their partners to meet the challenges of breast cancer.

The goal of this program is to help support you in your efforts as a couple to communicate more effectively and cope with the stressors associated with cancer. We also hope that by bringing couples together, all of whom share a similar experience, we will offer participants a support network and that couples will learn from each other. We hope to help both partners to work as a team to adjust to the changes brought about by cancer and to help each other to deal with distress.

Some weeks we will give you simple home assignments so that you may practice what you learn in sessions at home between sessions. You may find that some of the activities that we invite you to complete at home will be simple and fun whereas others may be more difficult. Since we have only a limited amount of time to meet together here, the program will be most beneficial if you continue to learn at home, between sessions. You might also discover that directly after attending these meetings or in the week between meetings you and your partner might discuss issues that were brought up in the group or other topics that group discussions made you think about. This is very common among couples attending these types of groups.

If for any reason, you feel distressed—depressed, highly anxious, have severe marital problems—or feel uncomfortable during the 6-week program, feel free to speak with either of the group leaders privately.

Each week one of the group leaders will serve as the timekeeper for the group. Since we have a lot of material to cover in a limited amount of time, it will be important for us to remain on schedule. The timekeeper will ensure that we are able to get through all the material—so she or he may stop you in the middle of an activity so that we can move on to the next topic. Please do not take it personally if he or she seems abrupt.

Next, make a statement regarding the importance of confidentiality in maximizing comfort in group participation. Assure participants that any recording or observation of the groups is regarded as confidential information and treated accordingly. Caution members to protect the anonymity of other group members as well. Similarly, tell participants that any questionnaires they complete will not contain any identifying information and will be safely stored to preserve their anonymity.

Although we cannot control what you might discuss when you leave this room, we would hope that what is said during our meetings remains in this room. As the leaders of the group, what you say to us is confidential unless we feel that you are a danger to yourself, to others, or to a child. Those are the three exceptions to confidentiality. Otherwise what you say here stays here. To protect your anonymity, any written questionnaires that you fill out will not contain your name or any other identifying information.

Getting to Know You Exercise (20 minutes)

To begin the icebreaker activity, invite couples to pair up and spend a few minutes getting to know another couple from the group by introducing themselves to that couple. If there is an uneven number of dyads, three couples can introduce themselves to each other. Ask participants to interview another couple as a way of letting others in the group know about who they are. Instruct couples as follows:

Please spend a few minutes getting to know another couple from the group and introducing yourself to that couple. This is a way of letting others in the group know a bit about who you are and what challenges and/or changes have been presented by the cancer. You are free to share as much or as little information as you feel comfortable with at this time.

Refer couples to the following sample interview questions in the workbook.

- How would the couple like to be addressed by other members of the group (first name, nickname, etc.)?

- How did the couple meet?

- How long have they been together?

- Do they have any children? If yes, how many, and how old are they?

- What details would they like to share about the cancer diagnosis?

- What is the current stage of treatment or when was treatment completed?

- Are there other things about themselves that they are interested in sharing with the group?

After a few minutes, invite all members to return to the group and ask each couple to introduce another couple to the group.

When introductions are completed, proceed to the subgroup discussion activity.

Patient Subgroup Discussion (15 minutes)

To begin the discussion of the impact of cancer on marital life, ask the patients with cancer to meet with either you or your coleader for a smaller, 15-minute group discussion. Arrange chairs so that the subgroup is demarcated, with members facing each other, but so that it can be easily seen and heard by everyone. Ask patients to talk with each other about the effect they think cancer has on them and their relationship with their partner. The question to focus the discussion is: *"What are your thoughts about the impact of cancer on you and your relationship with your partner?"*

In structuring this first subgroup discussion, be sure to clarify the structure and the roles of each leader to the group. It might be helpful for the subgroup discussion leader to say, as he or she sits down with the subgroup of patients, *"During this part of the meeting, we are going to speak with each other as if the others are not present."*

While the patients and their coleader engage in this discussion, the rest of the group members (the partners), along with the remaining coleader, are invited to observe and listen without interruption or reaction. The observer coleader might also reinforce this format by saying, *"We're going to strictly listen during this part. While you may notice your own thoughts and reactions to what is being said, it is important to try to really hear what it is that the others are expressing."*

The emphasis throughout this part of the session is on discussion between the group members *within* each subgroup and on encouraging both similar and contrasting points of view. Partners should become increasingly aware of differing perspectives within and between couples, and that the couple must take these differing viewpoints and feelings into account. Be sure to discourage cross-group discussion because such exchanges will interfere with the structural intervention intended by organizing members along illness-role lines rather than by couple membership. In highlighting shared perspectives across couples, differing attitudes and feelings are objectified and de-intensified within couples.

Encourage interaction between members of the subgroup and organize and summarize the subgroup's ideas, feelings, and impressions. You may want to talk with your coleader during the group about the different perspectives that are being expressed. Such discussions are often valuable ways to clarify issues for the group and to ensure that you and your coleader are together in your perceptions of what is being said by group members.

Two patterns often occur during the subgroup meetings. First, although there will be a tendency for the subgroup participants to talk primarily to the group leader, they should be encouraged to talk among themselves. This promotes group interaction and cohesiveness and supports the stated assumption that the couples themselves are the experts. Sometimes this has to be facilitated with questions such as, *"Has anyone else had a similar or a different experience?"* or *"What are other people's thoughts about what Staci had to say?"* Second, particularly initially, group members are often vague in describing the effects of cancer. Statements such as "I feel worried all the time" need to be made more specific. Questions such as *"Alicia, when do you notice yourself feeling particularly worried?"* or *"What is it about living with your husband that you find particularly worrisome these days?"* help participants relate these feelings to specific aspects of their lives.

The process of specifying illness-related problem areas has another important purpose. It diminishes the global and seemingly overwhelming quality of the feelings that come up in response to the cancer. This is particularly important during early phases of the group, when couples most fear that the discussions will stir up strong feelings about which nothing can be done.

Obviously, if you or your coleader intervenes too often to ask for specificity or clarification, the interactions will become focused on you. A useful strategy is to let the patients talk among themselves without interruption for 5 to 10 minutes while making mental notes of points to be clarified by the end of the subgroup discussion.

Patients usually have a lot to say, and the subgroup discussion usually includes some complaining and swapping of "war stories" about physicians or aspects of medical treatment. If these complaints become the sole focus of discussion, gently draw attention back to relationship issues by saying, *"We seem to have gotten away from how illness affects your lives in terms of your relationship. Mary, you were saying that you sometimes feel overprotected by your partner. How does that happen?"* It is most important, as a basic rule of thumb in all the group discussions in this program, to maintain a focus on the couple as a unit.

When the patient subgroup finishes its discussion (after approximately 15 minutes), the coleader might say, *"A number of important ideas and feelings have come up here. It's our turn to sit back and listen to the impressions of others."* Instruct the patients to observe and listen to their partners without interruptions or reactions.

At this point, the other (observer) coleader would say to his or her group, *"I'd like for you to reflect on what we have heard from the other group. What is it that each of you heard your partner and the other group members expressing?"* Partners talk among themselves, without input from the patient subgroup, for about 10 minutes. Encourage this partner subgroup to respond to each other's comments as well as to the patient subgroup. The group leader who is working with the partner group may draw connections between the various observations of different members and may begin to identify different marital themes that emerge in the discussion. Ask silent members for their ideas or impressions.

Without being overly rigid, the group leader working with the observers should help the group focus on relationship issues related to cancer. It is important to keep in mind that many families do not typically think or speak in terms of the "couple as a unit." Getting spouses or significant others to "speak for the couple" will probably take several meetings. Individuals will naturally tend to give their own opinions and feelings, but the group leaders should, from the first meeting, gently but consistently establish a focus on the couple as a unit facing and responding to the chronic demands of cancer. This focus on the part of the group leaders applies to all subgroup meetings and observer response discussions. No participant should be cut off or criticized for what he or she says but through respectful, interested questioning, be invited to share his or her perspective on the couple as a group.

Next, reverse the partner and patient roles, instructing the group:

> *The patients just had the opportunity to discuss how cancer has impacted their relationship, while the partners sat back and listened. Now, the partners are being given the opportunity to discuss what it has been like for them to be in a relationship with someone who has been diagnosed with and treated for cancer while their partners listen and observe.*

Partner Subgroup Discussion (15 minutes)

To begin the discussion of the impact of cancer on marital life among spouses, you or your coleader will ask the partners of the cancer patients to meet for a smaller, 15-minute group discussion. Again, arrange chairs so that the subgroup is demarcated, with members facing each other, but so that it can be easily seen and heard by everyone. Ask the male partners to talk with each other about the effect they think cancer has on them and their relationship with their partners. The question on which to focus the discussion is: *"What is it like for you in your marriage to be the partner of someone who has been diagnosed with and treated for cancer?"* The rest of the patient group members, along with the remaining coleader, are invited to listen without interruption.

In structuring this second subgroup discussion, be sure to clarify the structure and the roles of each leader to the group. It might be helpful for the subgroup discussion leader to say, as he or she sits down with the subgroup of partners, *"During this part of the meeting, we are going to speak with each other as if the others were not present."* The observer coleader might also reinforce this format by saying, *"We're going to strictly listen during this part. While you may notice your own thoughts and reactions to what is being said, it is important to try to really hear what it is that the others are expressing."*

Patient Feedback (10 minutes)

When the partner subgroup finishes its discussion (after approximately 15 minutes), the coleader might say, *"A number of important ideas and feelings have come up here. It's our turn to sit back and listen to the impressions of others."* The other (observing) coleader would at this point say to his or her patient group, *"I'd like for you to reflect on what we have heard from the other group. What is it that each of you heard your partner and the other group members expressing?"* The observers (patients) talk among themselves, without input from the partner subgroup, for about 10 minutes. Encourage the group to respond to each other's comments as well as to the partner subgroup. The group leader who is working with the observer group (patients) may draw connections between the various observations of different members of the group and may begin to identify different couple themes that emerge in the discussion. Silent members should be asked for their ideas or impressions.

Look for an appropriate point to tactfully stop the exercise and reconvene all members as one group for closing remarks.

You might then point out:

> *In the discussions in which you just participated, you may have noticed that the course of the discussion was somewhat different than the way in which you generally discuss issues at home. Not only did you have the opportunity to speak your thoughts without being interrupted, but you also were given the chance to practice listening without interrupting. This has been demonstrated to be a very effective means of communication among couples, and we will continue to practice taking turns speaking and listening over the course of the next several weeks.*

Feedback, Program Schedule, and Administrative Information (5 minutes)

Next, elicit feedback from participants regarding the first meeting. Focus the discussion on couples' expectations in joining the group and goals for the sessions. Encourage participants to ask any questions that have arisen as a result of the first meeting. You might say, *"Now we want to check in with everyone and see how everyone felt about tonight's group."*

- *What are your expectations in participating in the group?*

- *What are your goals for the sessions?*

- *Does anyone have any questions?*

At the very end of the session, handle any administrative issues and refer members to the administrative information in the workbook. Review the schedule of meetings and make changes, where possible, to ensure the attendance of all couples at all meetings. Emphasize that given the vast amount of information compressed into six sessions and the fact that each participant plays an important role in the success of the group, attendance is critical. Close the group by thanking the group members for their attendance and participation.

Chapter 4 | *Session 2*

(Corresponds to chapter 2 of the workbook)

Materials Needed

- Flipchart and markers

- Name tags

- Pens/pencils and paper

- Reading Signs of Stress worksheet

- Focused Breathing relaxation script

Session Outline

- Review previous session (10 minutes)

- Present material on cancer-related stress (30 minutes)

- Conduct the Reading the Signs of Stress exercise and have couples participate in the "Not-So-Newlywed Game" (30 minutes)

- Introduce relaxation techniques and lead group in Focused Breathing exercise (15 minutes)

- Assign homework (5 minutes)

Session Objectives

- To provide psychoeducation geared toward couples on the stress of dealing with cancer

- To introduce couples to the use of relaxation techniques

Review of Previous Session (10 minutes)

Open the group by eliciting participants' feedback regarding the first session and any discussion between partners that the session may have prompted in the intervening week. You may wish to check directly with any participant who does not provide feedback to ensure that no one is overly anxious, threatened, or hurt. For example, you or your coleader might inquire, *"After attending a group like last week's, it is common for people to have some reactions to the group. I am wondering if anyone would like to share their reactions to last week's group or share some of the thoughts or discussions you had during the trip home after last week's group or at any other time during the week."* If you observe that particular group members are quiet, encourage their participation by noting, *"Jane, I notice that you have not yet commented. Is there anything you would like to add?"*

What Is Stress? (30 minutes)

Next, introduce general, psychoeducational material regarding stress.

> *Last week you had the opportunity to express what it has been like for you in your relationships to go through cancer diagnosis and treatment. One common theme that surfaced in last week's discussion was the stress of the cancer experience. One of the most commonly reported challenges for any couple, particularly couples contending with a medical issue such as cancer, is managing stress.*

Explain to participants that in the next portion of the session, the group is going to examine stress in general and the special stresses caused by cancer. All members have heard the word "stress," but for the purpose of today's discussion, a common definition is needed. Ask the group if anyone can define stress. Write the definitions on the flipchart and encourage interactive discussion among members. You may use the following sample dialogue:

> *Stress is defined as a nonspecific response of the body to a demand on it. There is a lot to cancer that can increase stress. Cancer is a stressor that often demands a great deal of time and energy—physically and*

emotionally. Cancer diagnosis and treatment are stressful for the patient, the partner, and your relationship with one another, as well as other members of your family.

There are many stressful aspects of going through a cancer experience. Can anyone list some of the most challenging stresses that they have experienced?

Record responses on the flipchart and feel free to supplement participants' list of challenging stresses with the following:

- Treatment decisions

- Physical symptoms: pain, nausea, weakness, fatigue, etc.

- Changes in appearance: as a result of surgery, radiation, chemotherapy, etc.

- Hormonal side effects: such as hot flashes or premature menopause

- Limitations on ability to work: job, household chores, care for children/spouse

- Adjusting your normal household routine to accommodate treatment needs

- Managing finances

- Dealing with the impact on children

- Uncertainty about the future

Explain to the group that any one of the items just listed can be very stressful, and usually couples going through a cancer experience are dealing with more than one of these stressors. Also, the added demands of cancer may leave couples with little time or energy to attend to other demands in their daily lives, making it easy for stress to build up.

Talk about the different signs of stress. Some signs are obvious, like a pounding heart or butterflies in the stomach, but others are subtler. For instance, when some people are stressed, they may find it difficult to concentrate, or they may find that they misplace things like keys or important papers.

Ask the group to generate a list of some of the signs of too much stress. Write the following categories on the flipchart and ask the group to list signs for each.

Mental	Emotional	Physical	Relationships
Increased forgetfulness Difficulty concentrating	Depressed Anxious Irritable Hostile	Fatigue Headaches Muscle aches Sleep disturbance Stomach upset Appetite change	Poor communication Short fuse/temper Isolation

Continue the discussion by saying:

When one or both partners are experiencing stress, relationships can easily become "stressed" as well. When people feel stressed, they may have a "short-fuse," may become suddenly quiet, or may "take it out on their partners." These are all very common, yet not so helpful reactions.

As hard as it is to recognize stress in ourselves, it is even more difficult to recognize signs of stress in others. We can all learn to become better "stress detectives" by learning to identify stress in ourselves and in our partners so that we can respond to our own stress and help our partners respond to theirs. The first step is recognizing stress.

Reading the Signs of Stress Activity and the "Not-So-Newlywed Game" (30 minutes)

Explain to group members that they will participate in a game designed to help them better recognize stress in themselves and in their partners. Refer participants to the Reading the Signs of Stress worksheet in the workbook. Instruct them to write in the space provided the signs they can each identify when they are experiencing stress, as well as the signs they can identify when their partner is experiencing stress. Members should not share their responses with their partners. They will have the chance to share their respective lists with their partners and the group later in the session. Give the group 5 minutes to complete the worksheet.

After 5 minutes, have the group come back together and ask for a couple to volunteer to be the first "contestants" on the "Not-So-Newlywed Game." Have one partner volunteer to go first and read his or her list of the signs he or she can identify when his or her partner experiences signs of stress. Then, have the other partner read aloud his or her own signs of stress. Award one point to the couple for every sign of stress that they identified in themselves that corresponds to a sign that their partner identified in them. Have the rest of the group, who are observing, debate any questionable corresponding responses. For instance, if someone says that a sign of stress for him is "asking for attention" and his partner says he "asks for physical affection," let the group debate whether these two things correspond.

Instruct both partners in each couple to share their lists with each other and the group and then move on to another couple until all couples have completed the activity. Couples can keep track of their points in the space provided in their workbooks, or you can list them on the flipchart. After all the points are tallied, declare the winning couple the "Stress Detectives of the Week."

You may debrief the preceding exercise with the group by asking participants the following questions:

- *How well do you think you recognize the signs of stress in each other?*

- *What did you learn from playing the game?*

Ensure that each participant has an opportunity to comment. Then introduce the home assignment by stating:

> *Today we have discussed how stress affects us and our partners. We have discussed how cancer is stressful for both partners and how stress affects our relationships. It's important to remember that even though some couples scored more Stress Detective points than others in our "Not-So-Newlywed Game," each of us can work toward becoming a better Stress Detective within our relationship. The more aware you become of each other's stress reactions, the more you can understand and help each other to cope. For a home assignment, we want you all to review your completed Reading the Signs of Stress worksheets and discuss with your partner how stress affects both of you and your marriage. Use the questions in the workbook to guide your discussion.*

Ensure that group members understand the assignment and address any questions or issues raised by the group.

Focused Breathing Exercise (15 minutes)

Introduce the group to focused breathing, a relaxation technique helpful in coping with stress.

> *We are going to spend some time helping you learn relaxation techniques. One of the best ways to counter stress is to use relaxation techniques. It is a fact that our body has automatic physiological responses to stress (increased muscle tension, changes in breathing and heart rate, for instance). It is also a fact, proven by research, that we can counter these automatic stress responses through the use of relaxation techniques. Research has shown that such techniques not only counter our body's physiological stress response but also can leave you with a greater sense of mental calm and well-being.*

Explain to the group that relaxation takes time and practice. At first, it may seem very hard to do, and group members may not feel very good at it. Assure them that over time, and with practice, it will become easier and easier to reach a relaxed state more quickly. You may use the following sample dialogue:

> *Practicing relaxation techniques conditions your body to know what a relaxed state feels like and allows it to respond in this way more easily. Like exercise, the more you do it, the more your body becomes conditioned.*

> *When you try to focus on your breathing or a relaxing image, you may find that your mind wanders off to other things. This is natural. Our minds were made to think. When you catch your mind wandering, just let whatever thought you have go without evaluating it, and gently guide your focus back to the relaxation. As you do this more, it will become easier.*

> *It is helpful to start practicing relaxation techniques even at times when you're not feeling particularly stressed. In fact, practicing during lower stress times may make it easier to keep your mind focused and*

will allow you to get comfortable with the basics before being faced with a really stressful situation. You're like an athlete developing your skills before the "big game".

Tell participants that the first technique to be practiced is called passive relaxation or focused breathing (based on Davis, Eshelman, & McKay, 1982; Burish, Snyder & Jenkins, 1991; Benson, 1975; Loscalzo & Jacobsen, 1990). If they want, group members may close their eyes during the exercise. If they prefer to keep their eyes open, instruct them to pick an object or point in the room on which to focus. If they have a preference regarding the lights, you may adjust them accordingly.

The relaxation script follows.

Focused Breathing Script

Why don't you begin by finding a comfortable position. Slowly allow your body to unwind and just let it go. That's it. I wonder if you can allow your body to become as calm as possible . . . just let it go, just let your body sink into that chair. Feel free to move or shift around in any way that your body needs to, to find that comfortable position. You need not try very hard. Simply and easily allow yourself to follow the sound of my voice as you allow your body to find itself a safe, comfortable position to relax in.

If you like, you can gently allow your eyes to close; just let the lids cover your eyes. Allow your eyes to sink deeply, that's it, just let them go, falling back gently and deeply as your lids begin to feel heavier and heavier. As you allow your head to fall back deeply, feeling the weight of your head relaxing as you breathe out, just breathe out, one big breath. Slowly, if you can, turn your attention to your breathing. Notice your breath for a few moments, how much air you take in, how much air you let out, and just breathe evenly and naturally, and with the sound of my voice. I wonder if you can begin to take in more air, breathing in and out, in and out, that's it, gradually breathing in and out, breathing in calmness and quietness, breathing out tiredness and frustration, that's it. Let it go, it's not important to you now, breathing in quietness and control, breathing out fear and tension, breathing in and out, in and out.

You can enjoy breathing in this relaxed way for as long as you need to. You are peaceful now as you continue to observe your even and steady breathing that is allowing you to feel gentle and calm, breathing that is allowing you to feel a gentle calm, that's it, breathing relaxation in and tension out, in and out, breathing in quietness and control, breathing out tension and tiredness. That's it. As you continue to notice the quietness and stillness of your body, take a few quiet moments to experience this process more fully.

I am going to count backward from 5, and as I do, I'd like you to gradually become more aware of everything around you. Take in a final deep breath and—5—let it out. 4—begin to open or refocus your eyes. 3—begin to become more aware of the room around you. 2—notice the sense of calm that you have achieved remains with you as you take in your surroundings. And 1—notice how good it is to reconnect with everything around you, feeling more relaxed, calm, and refreshed.

Mark the end of the exercise by increasing the pace, raising the volume of your voice, and shifting positions.

Then, ask group members how they feel about the exercise and respond to any questions or concerns they may have. Let group members know that they are expected to practice focused breathing for homework. Partners may practice on their own or together as a couple. If they wish, they may take turns guiding each other through the exercise, or make their own audiotape of the exercise to use alone or together as a couple. Encourage couples to engage in focused breathing as often as possible over the course of the next week by saying:

You should also try to become more aware of ways in which you can encourage and support each other in practicing and using relaxation techniques. The more you practice this type of exercise, the more you will be able to do it naturally, without instructions. Feel free to practice this breathing exercise as many times as you wish throughout the week. We'll check in with everyone next session to see how this went for you.

Instructions for the breathing exercise, as well as a copy of the relaxation script, are included in each couple's workbook.

Homework (5 minutes)

✎ Ask couples to discuss their completed Reading the Signs of Stress worksheets with one another and answer the related discussion questions in the workbook.

✎ Instruct group members to practice the focused breathing technique as often as possible before the next meeting.

Chapter 5 | *Session 3*

(Corresponds to chapter 3 of the workbook)

Materials Needed

- Flipchart and markers

- Name tags

- Pens/pencils and paper

- Comfortable chairs and light controls for the relaxation exercises

- Progressive Muscle Relaxation script

- Copies of the American Cancer Society (ACS) brochure "Sexuality & Cancer: For the Woman Who Has Cancer and Her Partner" (See Chapter 2)

- 10 blank 3-by-5 index cards for each couple to use to create their Intimacy Deck

- Sensate Focus cards (See Chapter 2)

Session Outline

- Review homework (10 minutes)

- Introduce coping with stress material (10 minutes)

- Introduce material on physical affection and sexuality (10 minutes)

- Engage couples in role-play exercise and discuss group reactions (25 minutes)

- Have couples create an Intimacy Deck in session (15 minutes)

- Describe Sensate Focus (5 minutes)

- Conduct Progressive Muscle Relaxation exercise in group (10 minutes)

- Assign homework (5 minutes)

Session Objectives

- To introduce concept of Couple-Focused Coping to participants and offer couples suggestions for effectively taking care of themselves, each other, and their relationship

- To provide additional instruction in relaxation techniques

Homework Review (10 minutes)

To begin the group, summarize the focus of the previous group meetings and review the homework assignments. Try to facilitate feedback and discussion among group members.

Ask for feedback on the use of the Focused Breathing technique taught in the last session. Inquire how the practices went and whether or not members found them helpful. Assess barriers to using the technique among those who did not complete the home assignment and address these as a means of increasing future compliance.

Ask for general feedback regarding the Reading the Signs of Stress assignment and ask the following questions of the group:

- *How accurate were you in identifying signs of stress in your partner?*

- *How accurate was your partner in identifying signs of stress in you?*

- *Did your partner identify any signs that you did not think of or were not previously aware of in yourself or in your partner? Any surprises?*

- *What is the impact of stress on your relationship?*

- *What do you want from your partner when you feel stress?*

- *What does your partner want from you when he or she feels stress?*

Next, reintroduce the topic of coping with stress. While presenting the material to the group members, try to engage participants as much as possible. For instance, ask the members to describe how they cope with stress as a couple or to list ways in which a couple's intimate relationship may change as a result of coping with cancer. Remember to periodically ask participants if they have questions regarding the material being presented. You may use the following sample dialogue:

> *Today we are going to continue our discussion of ways to deal with stress. In this and the next few meetings we will be helping you and your partner find new or additional ways to relieve stress, to take care of yourselves and each other. Today we are going to talk about some strategies for coping with stress, including an additional relaxation technique. We are going to pay particular attention to ways in which you can combat the effects of cancer-related stress "as a couple."*

Coping With the Stress of Illness and Treatment (10 minutes)

Explain to the group that there are effective and less effective ways of coping with the stress of cancer treatment. It is important for all couples to become aware of any nonproductive coping responses that they may be using, even if they only use them once in a while. Ask participants if they can think of any nonproductive coping strategies. Supplement their responses with the following:

- Avoidance

- Sleeping too much

- Drinking too much

- Keeping things to yourself

- Denying what you feel, to yourself and others

Tell couples:

> *Instead of using these nonproductive strategies, it is important for each of us to have a "toolbox" filled with tools we can use to help our self and our partner cope with stress effectively.*

There are a number of different coping strategies that many couples find helpful when dealing with the experience of cancer.

Ask members if they can think of coping strategies that may be helpful in dealing with the stress of cancer and list responses on the flipchart. Be sure the following examples of productive coping strategies are included:

- Gathering information

- Seeking emotional support

- Distraction

- Seeking advice from a trusted friend, relative, or professional

- Relaxation techniques

- Expressing feelings

Continue the discussion by saying:

Each of the strategies that we have listed here may be helpful at certain times. The key to effective coping is identifying what part of a stressful situation you can change or control and then picking a coping strategy that will work best to deal with that aspect of the stress. When deciding how to approach a particular stress that you might encounter during the cancer experience, or at any time, there are a few simple steps that you can go through to determine what type of coping strategy might "fit" best.

Choosing the Right Coping Strategy

There are three steps to picking the right coping strategy for a particular situation. Write the steps on the flipchart and review with the group.

Step 1: Break down the stressor into something specific that you can work on. For example, do not try to deal with "being anxious," but instead work on "being anxious when I go for my treatment/checkup."

Step 2: Label aspects of the situation controllable or uncontrollable. For example, "I cannot control the fact that I have to go for my treatment/checkup (source of stressor), but I can work toward controlling my anxiety about being there (response to the stressor)."

Step 3: Decide on a coping strategy to help with controllable aspects. How are you going to tackle the stress? Will you use something like bringing your partner or your best friend along to the hospital for support, or listening to music to distract yourself? Will you try using relaxation techniques before or during the treatment/checkup?

Stress the importance of trying a variety of coping strategies, respecting individual differences in coping style, and providing coping suggestions to one's partner in a noncritical way. Encourage couples to try to use a number of different coping strategies. Stress the importance of trying new techniques until couples figure out what works best for them. You may use the following sample dialogue:

> *Try to use a number of different coping strategies. It is important to keep trying new techniques to care for yourself and your partner until you figure out what works best for you.*

> *Each couple and each individual is different. It is important to be respectful of the different coping styles that you and your partner may have. There may be times when you disagree with your partner's way of dealing with a stress. Remember, just as in other areas of your relationship, criticism of how someone is dealing with something is unlikely to bring the effect you desire. Our research with other couples has shown that criticizing how your partner is dealing with a situation can lead your partner to become more passive and avoidant in dealing with the stressful situation, which can lead to more distress.*

> *Rather than criticizing what your partner is doing or not doing, try to express your concern for your partner and your relationship, and make suggestions for other ways of coping in a sensitive and caring manner.*

Physical Intimacy and Sexuality (10 minutes)

You may use the following sample dialogue to introduce the material:

> *We have spent a fair amount of time in the past weeks discussing stress. You have probably become more familiar with your own stress reactions*

as well as those of your partner. You may have even begun to recognize how stress affects your relationship. Stress, in particular the stress of coping with cancer, can impact a couple's relationship in many ways.

A specific area of a couple's relationship that may be affected by cancer and its treatment is that of physical affection and sexual intimacy. Sexual concerns are not uncommon among women with breast cancer and their partners. However, despite the high frequency of sexual concerns, these concerns are often difficult to discuss with your partner or others. We want you to know that you are free to discuss any of your concerns in the group; however, we understand that this is sometimes difficult for people to discuss openly, and we will not pressure you to contribute your thoughts.

Role-Play and Discussion (25 minutes)

Use the following case vignette to engage couples in a role-play exercise. You may wish to photocopy the dialogue provided and distribute to couples so they can role play the sample conversation. One partner can play the role of the patient, and the other can play the role of the spouse/significant other. You or your coleader can play the role of the therapist. In deciding whom to have participate in this exercise, you might first ask for volunteers, and then nominate the couple who has been most verbal in the sessions. Introduce the role-play as follows:

The following example depicts a couple (Lisa and John) talking to their therapist about the impact the wife's breast cancer and subsequent mastectomy and reconstructive surgery have had on their marriage.

Lisa (to John): I had concerns when they said I had to have my breast removed. I was worried about how you would see my body. I had concerns about how you would look at me and if you would still think I'm attractive.

John (to Lisa): It didn't make any difference to me that you had lost a breast or that you had reconstructive surgery. I am in love with you, not your breasts, just as you are in love with me and not my body. Things happen in life that you can't control, but that doesn't mean our relationship has to change.

Therapist: It's natural for a woman who has gone through what you have gone through—a mastectomy and then reconstruction—to worry about how your partner is going to view your body and to worry about feeling less attractive to one's partner.

Lisa (to therapist): There were times that I would think that a response from him was negative, when in fact it was a reflection of my own negativity. I would check with him time and time again to make sure that he wasn't rejecting me or being turned off by my body. Any little thing he said or did, I interpreted as meaning something else, something negative, so I had to keep checking and checking.

Therapist: One of the difficulties is that we fall into the trap of thinking that if my partner loves me, cares about me, knows me, he or she will be able to read my mind.

Lisa (to therapist): I was afraid of losing him. I was afraid that if I wasn't there, in every sense, especially when it came to sex, that our marriage would be over.

John (to Lisa): I can understand how you might feel. But really, I am so happy you are alright, and I am still as attracted to you as ever. I hope you understand that.

Lisa (to John): I understand, and I am really glad to hear that you feel this way.

Therapist: When we don't express our vulnerability to our partners, I think we rob our partners of an opportunity to show their love, their concern, and their caring for us.

Lisa (to therapist): I don't care how long you are married to someone. You just don't know how they are going to react to something like this. Each time I let him see me, or those times when I just couldn't be with him intimately, I would think, this is it. This is going to be the last straw for him.

Therapist: The reality of cancer is that it disrupts a couple's normal lifestyle in every way, including your sex life. Chemotherapy and radiation treatments, as well as early morning doctor appointments, can cause fatigue, and it may be that neither of you is able to make love because you're both so tired. Also, sometimes surgical scarring and pain make having sex uncomfortable. You have to restructure things and think about different ways to maintain physical intimacy.

Lisa (to therapist): I remember saying to him that I sometimes thought that my sexual desire might never come back, that I would think to myself, "Will we ever go back to the way we used to be?"

Therapist: One way for you to get around that feeling is to give yourself permission to be less spontaneous. It's OK to say, "I can't right now, but once I take my nap I'll be ready." It doesn't mean that your relationship is going down the tubes if you don't engage in spontaneous lovemaking like you did earlier in your relationship. It's one of the accommodations that have to be made.

Lisa (to therapist): What I responded to was to his persistence—not to being sexual, but to being open. He encouraged me to continue our relationship the way it had been before, even if in a limited fashion. He didn't do this in a pushy way. He has just been very patient with me. I'm certain that there were times when I rejected his advances and in a very loving way he would just continue to come and, the way he did before, stroke me, and that's when it would kind of surprise me that he would even want to touch that lump, my breast.

Therapist: It's normal to wonder, "How can my partner find me attractive if I look so different?" It is also normal to not feel desirable after being diagnosed with breast cancer.

Lisa (to partner): You looked at me exactly the same way. I never saw you shy away from looking at me. And I have to say that when I looked in the mirror and saw my chest, I would wish that I could have my old body back. I wanted that for both of us, not just for me, but you don't seem to have any desire to have me any way other than the way I am.

Therapist: Sometimes it's not the partner who withdraws, but the cancer patient who says, "I don't feel attractive so I'm not in the mood." Keep in mind that a lot of our sexuality is how we feel about ourselves, how sexy we feel within our own imaginations. So I think that one of the main concerns is, "Will I still be attractive?"

The best thing you can do is keep the lines of communication open. It's not easy to do, but it's important, especially during this time in your lives. You have to share your needs with one another. If you don't, it's impossible for either of you to understand what each of you is going through. It's also important that you have other people to talk to, people who can help. Whether it be your medical doctor or your therapist, it's helpful to have people to turn to when you have questions.

Lisa: Right now I have a couple of problems. I feel some pain and discomfort in my breast that I didn't have before. Sometimes I feel disconnected from my body, like it's not real because of the reconstruction. It helps that he has a gentle way of approaching me, of touching me. He gives me back rubs, and he's very tender and understanding when it hurts. I'm learning day by day that by responding to him and focusing more on how I feel in my mind and not in my body, I feel more comfortable, and the discomfort isn't as intense. Still, I'm wondering if I can do more to ease my pain. How long will it last?

Therapist: What I'm hearing you say is that the sexuality between you and your husband has now become a more sensual kind of experience, so that you do a lot more touching and holding and caressing. However, the pain is still distressing.

Lisa (to therapist): Right. The reconstruction has left me a little numb. It's an uncomfortable feeling. The pressure of his body on my chest now is disconcerting to me, it takes away the intimacy because it hurts or it's unfamiliar. I don't know if you can imagine what it feels like to lean up against something and you don't feel anything—my whole abdomen is that way.

Therapist: Well, this is something you should talk to your medical doctor about, although I can say that your experience is pretty typical of women who have had reconstructive surgery. Over time, these sensations will become more familiar, and you will regain sensitivity.

Lisa (to therapist): I see. I'll call my doctor tomorrow. It's good to have someone to talk to about the physical aspect of the cancer. This way, I can communicate better with my husband.

Therapist: Great. Let me wrap up by saying that couples who are coping with breast cancer can still have a healthy sex life. Sexuality and intimacy can be expressed in many different ways. Just sharing a special moment can be a real sexual experience for a lot of people. Look at yourselves and your relationship and find out what you need to do as a couple to develop that sense of sexuality.

Lisa: I'd like to say that today I feel very positive. I don't see my situation in a negative way any more.

After engaging couples in the role-play, open the floor for discussion. Ask couples for their reactions to the role-play and the dialogue between Lisa and John. Ask whether they can relate to the issues presented (e.g., concerns about appearance, physical pain and fatigue, fear of abandonment).

Even though participants may be uncomfortable discussing intimate concerns in the group format, you and your coleader should encourage participant-generated discussion but should not push quiet group members to speak. Proceed with lecture material, allowing for questions and comments from participants. You may use the following sample dialogue:

> We're going to spend the next few minutes talking about some of the direct and indirect effects of cancer on sexual functioning and satisfaction. We will also provide you with information that you, as a couple, can use to cope with such issues. At the end of the session, we will give each couple a booklet, published by the American Cancer Society, that discusses the impact of cancer on physical intimacy. Many couples find this booklet to be quite informative.

Point out that although much of the discussion about sexuality and cancer focuses on the direct impact of cancer on the patient, it is not unusual for partners to experience sexual concerns as well. Partners may feel excessively concerned about hurting the patient, whether by expressing sexual interest and being seen as demanding, or by causing physical pain during intimacy. These fears may affect the partner's desire and sexual performance. Whether concerns about sexuality are on the part of the woman treated for breast cancer or her partner, they are important for the couple to address.

Treatment for breast cancer can raise several potential barriers to resuming and maintaining sexual intimacy. List these for the group.

- Direct effects of illness and treatment such as pain, fatigue, and time constraints

- Emotional distress: anxiety, depression, disappointment, and fear

- Avoidance and lack of communication between partners

- Beliefs that sexual activity is unsafe during and after cancer treatment

In order to resume and maintain an affectionate, intimate relationship, women with breast cancer and their partners may need to address several issues. Discuss the following issues in detail.

1. Coping with changes in appearance and rebuilding sexual self-esteem

   - Cancer treatment often results in visible changes to the breast as well as a woman's overall body image (e.g., weight gain, weight loss).
   - It is common for individuals to underestimate their physical attractiveness and to focus on what they find unattractive in themselves.
   - Partners can help us feel more secure in our sexuality by making positive statements about our appearance or other sexual qualities.
   - Patients and partners often need to acknowledge the loss of the breast (in mastectomy), or the presence of a scar (in lumpectomy), in the process of grieving and psychological recovery.

2. Anxiety related to sexual performance

   - Feeling relaxed is important for sexual comfort and pleasure.
   - Partners can engage in techniques, both individually and as a couple, to promote sexual comfort.
   - Spend time with your partner in ways that focus on physical pleasure and intimacy without the expectations of sexual performance.

3. Applying good communication skills

   - Miscommunication about sexual concerns can result from mind reading, trying to protect your partner, etc.
   - Express concerns and identify support preferences by applying good speaking and listening skills.
   - If a partner becomes distant because of worries or fears but does not openly communicate these concerns, women with breast cancer may mistakenly believe the partner is reacting to her altered appearance.

- Physical communication and closeness can be simple—as simple as holding hands, hugging, and cuddling.
- Communication with medical staff or other experts may also be important in dealing with concerns about physical intimacy. Tell couples:

By discussing your intimate concerns with your physician, you may receive information, suggestions, or recommendations to help you overcome these issues. If you feel you will be nervous in bringing up this topic with your doctor, you may want to write down your concerns and bring them with you to your appointment. This might help you to feel less anxious and remind you to address these issues during your visit with the doctor.

Negotiation of a Revised Sexual Script

Introduce couples to the concept of a "sexual script." You may use the following sample dialogue:

A sexual script is the blueprint that guides our intimate expectations and sexual encounters. Your intimate relationship will likely experience some changes after cancer diagnosis and treatment. The effects of cancer and cancer treatment (such as fatigue, pain, etc.) may make it necessary to change some features of your sexual script (such as time of day, sexual position, spontaneity, etc.). Sometimes an individual or a couple may feel that changing aspects of their "sexual script" means that this part of their life will no longer be as satisfying. They may focus on wanting it "the way it used to be." It's important to remember, though, that "the way it used to be" was probably "fun, pleasurable, and close." With some necessary adjustments, it can be that way again.

Cancer treatment demands a great deal of time and is physically and emotionally demanding. Oftentimes, couples become caught up in cancer treatment and have a difficult time remembering to tend to their own and their partner's emotional needs. You may feel closer to each other after this experience, or more distant. You may spend a lot of time together coping with the illness, and these tasks may interfere with your time together as a couple. It is important to make time to engage in pleasurable activities as a couple and to make these activities priorities in your busy schedules.

The Intimacy Deck (15 minutes)

During this part of the session, couples will create something called an Intimacy Deck. This is a deck of cards where each card lists an enjoyable activity that couples can do together. You may use the following sample dialogue to introduce the concept of the Intimacy Deck:

> *We are going to ask you to create an Intimacy Deck composed of several activities that you and your partner can enjoy together as a couple. These can be activities that you've done in the past or things you've thought about doing. An activity may be very simple, or it may be more involved. For example, you may identify simply making dinner together, taking a short walk in the neighborhood, or listening to a special song together as pleasurable activities. Your ideas may be more elaborate, such as creating a special gourmet meal together or going to a concert together. Some activities may help create a romantic mood; others may be sheer laughter and playfulness. These can all lead to a greater sense of closeness between the two of you.*

Give couples a few minutes to discuss their ideas. Guide them through the following steps for creating their Intimacy Deck.

Step 1: Brainstorm

> *Let your imagination and experience be your guides in suggesting the most interesting and enjoyable things to do together. Consider all your ideas, no matter how foolish they sound; you never know—the most foolish ideas just might be the most fun! Remember the rule of brainstorming: Never be negative about any suggestion, no matter how silly it seems.*

Step 2: Collaborate

Talk to each other about the experiences that you think will be the most pleasurable for both of you, and then decide which experiences you will include in your Intimacy Deck. Pick activities that you may actually have the means to carry out even though some planning may be involved. Write each activity on a separate card.

Give each couple a deck of note cards/index cards and pens/pencils to create their Intimacy Deck. Allow about 10 minutes for this exercise. Reconvene the group and spend a few minutes on the remainder of this activity. Elicit feedback by asking the following questions.

- *How did you do in creating an Intimacy Deck?*

- *Are there any ideas you'd like to share with the group?*

- *What did you learn about your partner in thinking up activities for your Intimacy Deck?*

After this brief discussion, let the group know that there is a third step to follow.

Step 3: Do it!

Many of the world's greatest ideas remain ideas because they are never put into action. Once you decide to try something, don't wait; do it now or at least make the plans and set aside a time when you will do it.

As one of your home assignments before the next session, engage in at least one activity from your Intimacy Deck.

Sensate Focus (5 minutes)

Next, introduce the Sensate Focus card to the group. This is a card that you will hand out and that couples should include in their Intimacy Decks (see Chapter 2). You may use the following sample dialogue to introduce this new activity card:

We're sure that each couple here today has come up with some very special, personal cards to include in their Intimacy Deck. We are also going to "stack the deck" by giving each couple here an additional card to add to the deck that you have created.

Distribute the Sensate Focus card to each couple.

This card is entitled "Sensate Focus." This activity is intended to increase that feeling of "connection" between you and your partner. We are going to ask you to complete the activity on this card, in addition to one other that you choose from your Intimacy Deck, in the next week.

Explain Sensate Focus in more detail and make sure all group members understand the activity.

We would like for you to make some quiet, private time where you can relax and simply focus on being together. We would like for you to take turns touching, caressing, and massaging each other in an intimate but nonsexual way. Both partners should be fully clothed—wearing whatever clothing they find comfortable. One partner should focus on the other by touching and caressing different body parts like the shoulders, face, hands, and legs without touching the genital region or the breasts (in the case of the women). The person who is giving the massage should try different ways of stroking their partner with different amounts of pressure, asking their partner to provide feedback about what feels best and responding to that. The partner who is being caressed should gently say what feels good, what might feel better, what they like most. It is very important to phrase all feedback to your partner in a positive way. For example, instead of saying, "That doesn't feel good," or "Don't rub so hard," say "It would feel even better if you did _____," or "I'd really like you to continue that with lighter pressure." Make sure to tell your partner when something feels good!

The aim of this exercise is not to lead to further sexual activity. The aim is to create closeness through physical touch, to learn to communicate your physical preferences to your partner, and to understand your partner's physical needs.

You may complete Sensate Focus as many times as you wish throughout the week. Make sure that each of you gets to touch and be touched as well.

After presenting the Intimacy Deck and Sensate Focus tasks, ask if any group members have questions about the material. If there are questions, briefly address them before moving on.

Progressive Muscle Relaxation (PMR) (10 minutes)

Last week, the group practiced Focused Breathing. This week, you will introduce the second relaxation exercise—Progressive Muscle Relaxation (PMR). This technique incorporates the tensing and releasing of muscles in order to decrease feelings of stress. Instruct participants to find a comfortable position in their chairs, and then use the following script to facilitate the relaxation exercise.

PMR Script

Gradually allow your body to be still . . . you may move around and adjust your body in any way that you like until your body finds itself in a comfortable position. Gently guide your focus to a point in the room, and if you like, allow your eyes to close. Slowly begin to focus your attention inward, tuning out any outside noises or distractions; they are not important to you now. Simply and easily allow your body to sink deeper and deeper into your chair. Just continue breathing normally . . . breathing in and out . . . in and out . . . breathing in quietness and relaxation . . . breathing out tiredness and tension, breathing them right out of you.

Allow your mind to focus inward, gradually becoming aware of how your body feels. Now, I wonder if you can do a mental scan of your body. Notice how it feels. Are there any parts that are more relaxed than others? Any parts that feel more tight or tense than others? Any parts that need special attention?

Now I wonder if you can clench your hands into fists, tense your arms as you squeeze in your fingers tighter and tighter . . . and now just let them go. Once more now, make fists, tight fists, hold them, and then let them go. Now I wonder if you can lift up your shoulders, lift them up to your ears, hold them there. Squeeze them tightly, squeeze. And then let them drop down, just let them go . . . and then once more lift them up . . . hold it . . . then let them go . . . as you feel all the tightness and tension in your shoulders begin to drain away. . . . Now I wonder if you can release the tension in your face by squeezing your eyelids tightly, raising the corners of your mouth, pushing your tongue to the roof of your mouth, and clenching your jaw . . . squeeze as tightly as you can and then let it go. Once more, tighten all the muscles in your face, squeezing and clenching tightly, and then let them go, feeling the tension in your face draining away. Feel your head becoming more and more relaxed, allowing all the tension and tightness to drift out of it . . .

Now I wonder if you can tense up every muscle in your body . . . that's it, squeeze in the muscles . . . hold it, and just let it go . . . once more, tense up your muscles, make them very tight and tense, hold it, hold it . . . and then breathe out, and let your muscles relax, just let them go.

Slowly let your mind scan your body for any remaining tension. If there are any parts of your body that are still holding tension, take the next few seconds to tense the muscles in this area, hold it, and then let it go. Let all the tension go. And as you continue to breathe in calm and quiet, take a few moments to enjoy the fact that your body feels less tense than just a few minutes ago . . . that in this very brief time you have become more relaxed.

I am going to count backward from 5 and as I do, I'd like you to gradually become more aware of everything around you. Take in a final deep breath and—5—let it out. 4—begin to open or refocus your eyes. 3—begin to become more aware of the room around you. 2—notice the sense of calm that you have achieved remains with you as you take in your surroundings. And 1—notice how good it is to reconnect with everything around you feeling more relaxed, calm, and refreshed.

Inform the group members that they will be asked to practice this technique during the week as a home assignment. Instructions for the exercise, as well as the preceding relaxation script, are included in each group member's workbook. Explain to participants that practice is key to using relaxation effectively. Be sure to stress that the more often they practice, the better their bodies will become at responding to the technique.

Before ending the session, be sure to distribute the American Cancer Society brochures to couples and answer any outstanding questions they may have. Then, assign homework.

Homework (5 minutes)

✎ Instruct couples to engage in at least one pleasurable activity from their Intimacy Deck during the course of the next week.

✎ Couples should also engage in the Sensate Focus exercise at least once, making sure that each partner gets a chance to touch and be touched.

✎ Ask group members to practice PMR at least twice before next week's meeting.

✂

Sensate Focus Instructions

Sensate Focus is a simple activity that is intended to help you feel more connected to your partner.

Make some quiet, private time where you can relax and simply focus on being together.

Both of you should be fully clothed—wearing whatever clothing you find comfortable.

Take turns touching, caressing, and massaging each other in an intimate but nonsexual way.

One partner should focus on the other by touching and caressing different body parts like the hands, face, shoulders, and legs <u>without</u> touching the breasts (if you are touching your female partner) or the genital region. Try different ways of stroking your partner with different amounts of pressure, allowing for your partner to provide feedback about what feels best and responding to that.

The person who is being caressed should gently instruct the partner—let your partner know what feels good, what might feel better, what you like most. It is very important to <u>phrase all feedback to your partner in a positive way.</u> For example, instead of saying, "That doesn't feel good," or "Don't rub so hard," say, "It would feel even better if you did...," or "I'd really like you to continue that with lighter pressure." <u>Make sure to tell your partner when something feels good!</u>

The aim of this exercise is not to lead to further sexual activity. The aim is to create closeness through physical touch, to learn to communicate your physical preferences to your partner, and to understand your partner's physical needs.

You may complete Sensate Focus as many times as you wish throughout the week.

Make sure that each of you gets to touch and be touched as well.

Directions for Group Leaders: The Sensate Focus instructions are to be photocopied, cut out, and attached to index cards or printed on cardstock, and distributed to each couple in the group during Session 3.

Chapter 6 | *Session 4*

(Corresponds to chapter 4 of the workbook)

Materials Needed

- Flipchart and markers

- Name tags

- Pens/pencils and paper

- Case vignettes of couples using different methods of communication

- Visual aid representing "the floor" available for couples to use, if they wish, during the Speaker/Listener exercise

- Guided Imagery Relaxation script

Session Outline

- Review homework (10 minutes)

- Lead interactive discussion on communication, making sure to talk about the differences between good and bad communication (15 minutes)

- Review case vignettes depicting conversations between breast cancer patients and their partners (20 minutes)

- Introduce Speaker/Listener Technique and have couples practice the technique (30 minutes)

- Conduct Guided Imagery Relaxation exercise (10 minutes)

- Assign homework (5 minutes)

Session Objectives

- To introduce basic communication concepts and skills

- To enhance relaxation skills through the use of guided imagery

Homework Review (10 minutes)

At the start of the meeting, ask group members about their experiences with the home assignments. Elicit feedback regarding the Intimacy Deck activity. You may use the following questions to guide the discussion:

- *Would anyone care to share the activity they chose to complete from their Intimacy Deck?*

- *What was it like to do these activities together?*

- *What were the barriers to completing this activity?* (Ask this question if any couple did not complete the assignment)

Also inquire about participants' reactions to the Sensate Focus activity using the following questions to guide the discussion:

- *What was it like to complete the Sensate Focus exercises with your partner?*

- *What did you learn about yourself and your partner during this activity?*

Also check in with members on their use of the relaxation technique. You may use the following questions to guide the discussion:

- *How did your practice of the Progressive Muscle Relaxation go?*

- *Has anyone tried using the Progressive Muscle Relaxation or Focused Breathing techniques in a stressful situation? How did that go?*

Next, lead an interactive discussion on communication issues.

Issues of Communication (15 minutes)

One of the group leaders might begin the discussion by saying:

In the course of these discussions and activities you have probably noticed that there are some issues on which you and your partner agree, while there are others on which you disagree. Tonight we are not going to focus on which things you agree or disagree about, rather, we are going to discuss how you communicate as a couple about various issues. Communication is always important in any close relationship, but when couples are dealing with a very serious stressor like a cancer diagnosis, it becomes especially crucial. Communication is especially important for several reasons.

First, good communication between partners is important because it influences the way the patient ends up dealing with her illness and can influence how well the patient feels she is coping. A more supportive spouse and an open line of communication between patient and partner can encourage the patient to be a really active participant in her treatment, and a less supportive partner can end up (probably without realizing it) encouraging more avoidant or passive ways of dealing with the illness and thus lead to more distress.

Second, how partners communicate is very closely related to both marital satisfaction and how satisfied partners are with the support provided by their partners. Good communication leads to the patient feeling loved and supported, while poor communication can lead to feelings of abandonment and loneliness. Knowing how to communicate well can thus reduce both partners' distress during cancer treatment.

As important as communication is to couples coping with cancer, dealing with cancer often requires communication about tough topics with which you may have little prior experience. Communication can be difficult, and sometimes things get in the way of good communication.

Good Communication

Discuss the elements of good communication with the group. Good communication is when the message the speaker intended to send is accurately understood. That is, the intent (message sent) equals the impact (message received). Write this on the flipchart.

Talk about the two levels of a message. There is the verbal level, what is actually said, and there is the nonverbal level, how something is said and the emotional tone of the conversation. Explain that although a person may clearly state his or her thoughts and feelings, they may be hidden by the nonverbal style of the statements.

Despite their best efforts, couples sometimes do not communicate effectively. Ask couples if they can think of some reasons for this. Record their responses on the flipchart and organize them according to the following categories:

- Physical filters: examples include fatigue, pain, and noise

- Emotional filters: examples include depression, anger, anxiety, and fear

- Communication styles: examples include a wordy style, a rational style, or a flowery, emotional style

Explain to the group that communication difficulties can arise at any time due to communication styles and other filters.

> *Effective communication can be particularly challenging when couples are discussing a topic of disagreement or when criticism is being expressed. Even in the best of relationships, there are things that couples disagree about and times when we need to let our partner know how we feel about something he or she said or did. There are more and less effective ways of providing critical feedback or discussing personal differences with your partner.*

Present the following material, allowing for group participation. You may wish to draw two columns on the flipchart—one labeled "Destructive Communication" and one labeled "Constructive Communication." Begin by asking couples, *"What gets in the way of good communication for you and your partner?"* Encourage discussion among group members and generate a list of participants' responses. Write the responses on the flipchart, making sure to put each one in the appropriate column.

After listening to couples input, you may wish to add the following examples of destructive communication patterns to the flipchart. You might say, *"Here are some examples of the most common destructive communication patterns. These are patterns in which couples frequently get stuck. Has anyone observed any of these patterns?"*

Destructive Communication Patterns

Summarizing self syndrome

- Saying your own point of view repeatedly
- *Not* listening to your partner's viewpoint

Cross-complaining

- Giving a complaint in response to a complaint

Kitchen-sinking

- Dragging other gripes into the talk, especially ones unrelated to the original issue

Yes, but . . .

- Superficially agreeing (but not really listening) followed by a return to your own position

The Standoff

- Each partner stands firm in own position, unwilling to see value in her or her partner's point of view
- Thinking: "If my partner just saw the reasonableness of my position, everything would be all right."
- Thinking: "If I give in, something terrible will happen."
- Seeing communication as a win-lose situation

Mind Reading

- Assuming you know what your partner is thinking, feeling, or intending

Insults or character assassinations

■ Sarcasm, name-calling, put-downs

Catastrophic interpretations

■ Statements such as "You always . . . " or "You never . . . "

Blaming

■ Blaming partner for relationship issues and problems

After listing the preceding examples, ask group members for ideas on what can be done to make these destructive communication patterns constructive and more effective.

> *There are more effective ways of expressing disagreement or critical feedback to your partner. Does anyone have ideas on what can make such communication constructive and more effective?*

Present the following material, allowing for group participation and listing points on the easel or board under the "Constructive Communication" column.

> *Constructive communication is when you effectively express your own thoughts and feelings while also showing respect for the other person.*

> *When expressing a disagreement or a criticism to one's partner, it is important to remember some common courtesies. There are several dos and don'ts of courteous, constructive communication that will help you effectively express yourself while remaining respectful of your partner. (Refer participants to the Common Courtesies for Effective Communication in the workbook.) Putting these guidelines into practice when you are expressing disagreement or criticism means doing a bit of mental work called "editing" in which you decide between several things to say and do, and pick the one that is most effective.*

The Don'ts	The Dos
Don't complain or nag	Give sincere and positive appreciation. If you have issues to resolve, schedule a time to hash things out
Don't hog the conversation	Express interest in your partner's views; try to listen; ask questions
Don't suddenly interrupt	Give your partner a chance to finish speaking
Don't put your partner down	Say things that you honestly feel, emphasizing how the specific behavior impacts you
Don't put yourself down	Identify specific behaviors, not character faults
Don't bring up old resentments	Focus on the present situation
Don't say what you cannot do or what you don't want to do	Say what you *can* do and what you *want* to do
Don't think only of your needs and desires	Think of your partner's needs and desires; be empathetic

After reviewing the guidelines, refer participants to the section in the workbook that deals with expressing criticism using the X-Y-Z Technique.

In the case when it is necessary to provide critical feedback, it is most beneficial to make criticism specific to a certain behavior or situation. Your partner will be more likely to receive criticism when you criticize what he is doing, not who they are. One way of doing this is to use the X-Y-Z Technique.

Demonstrate the X-Y-Z Technique using a simple example such as, *"When you ignore me by watching television when I am asking you a question, I feel hurt."* Explain to the group that using this technique allows for a better chance of initiating discussion than a global put-down such as "You are so self-involved!"

Be sure to mention that the X-Y-Z Technique can also be used to express appreciation to another person. It is not only useful for providing criticism.

Case Examples and Discussion (20 minutes)

At this point in the session, present the following case examples of breast cancer patients and their partners discussing various issues. These vignettes are real and based on actual conversations from couples who participated in a study of this group therapy program. You may wish to photocopy the case examples and distribute them to the group. You may also choose to have couples engage in role-plays based on the following conversations. Introduce the examples as follows:

> *We are going to review several case vignettes that illustrate some of the destructive and constructive communication patterns that we have discussed. These examples are based on actual conversations of couples coping with breast cancer.*

Case Vignette 1

In this first example, a husband is expressing critical feedback to his wife, which leads them to a conversation about household management. Please note: W represents wife and H represents husband.

W: *What do you think? You felt we had a difficulty in some respects?*

H: *Yeah—yes, sometimes you get very quickly irritated if I criticize you on something you seem to be quite sensitive about, and then you get defensive, and then you get angry and that kind of shuts things down.*

W: *Like what?*

H: *The issue of clutter, for example. You'll say things like, "I know, I know, all right!" You know, like I'm not supposed to continue talking with you. Um, that's one example.*

W: *Well, what can you say about it? I mean I need two or three years to work on it.*

H: *Well, that's not the point. The point is to discuss it so we can get going and do something about it.*

W: *OK, OK, then, so when I say, Jim, we need you to take off some time, you know when you have some free time, we'll both get together and we'll straighten up the basement . . .*

H: *Yeah?*

W: *Yes? And what happens? You find all kinds of other things to do! So, you know, you're putting it on me. How about you?? You're saying I won't discuss clutter, and yet you say, and yet the basement is cluttered and—*

H: *Oh, OK . . .*

W: *When I say, "Let's work on it," do you discuss it with me? And do you cooperate in doing anything about it? You find other things to do. Like you'll say, "We haven't been to Longwood Gardens for a while," or "I have to do this financial stuff," or "I have to go to the garden and take the stuff out to the compost and gee that takes a long time . . ."*

H: *You know what I think when I talk about clutter, what I have more in my mind is the piles of newspapers and magazines, and guess who I think is responsible for that?*

W: *(laughter) Oh, you don't have any piles, right?*

H: *Oh, as a matter of fact I do. Yeah, I mean if you want to play touché, you can keep it on that one.*

W: *Yeah, OK, but what good would a discussion do? (laughter) What would a discussion accomplish? I think we've been through it. And like you say about criticizing, you'll say, "Oh, do you know what? I came in and all the radios in the house were on . . ."*

H: *. . . radios and lights . . . or TVs . . .*

W: *or "You know you left the light on."*

H: *"You didn't turn the heat down."*

W: *That's your job! (laughter)*

H: *Well, it hasn't been officially stated as such.*

W: *No, but it kind of is.*

H: *But you've never made that clear.*

W: *Mmm—OK (skeptical look)*

Discuss the preceding vignette with the group and ask members if anyone can identify the type of communication portrayed. Supplement the group conversation with the following summary.

Summary

In this example, both partners are critical of the other and deflect their own part in the problem or responsibility for a solution by blaming the other. The wife uses sarcasm and derails the conversation with cross-complaints and kitchen-sinking. The discussion does not progress toward any type of compromise or solution.

Case Vignette 2

In the next segment, a couple is discussing the issue of household management. Encourage the group to observe the differences from the prior segment.

W: Well, um, I just want to say, a big worry in my life is that of the household tasks and how much is not getting done by me or by you and what we can do about it, because it's getting to be a big problem. And I know you have given me so much time and, uh, doing the shopping and helping with cooking, and the yard area, and so I feel guilty in requesting more help from you, and yet I'm not really able to do all the things that need to be done, and we need to work something out so more gets accomplished.

H: OK, so you're talking about general household tasks such as dusting, vacuuming, and things of that nature which I don't do and you've complained about any number of times, and right at the moment you're also talking about yard upkeep, upkeep of lawn and shrubs and so on.

W: [nods]

H: OK. What you've said is correct, there has been neglect in these areas, uh, my neglect about this situation is centered on the fact that, as you know, I don't like to dust and I'm not too keen on vacuuming, and we have, however, discussed more than once, about the fact that maybe we should hire someone to come in several hours a week and do some of the heavy cleaning around the house. And all we do is talk about it, but we don't really act on it.

W: Right.

H: And maybe we're both at fault in that.

W: Yeah, I accept some of that blame too. I just talk about it and complain about it.

H: Are we going to continue just talking about it, or are we serious about having someone come in? I know for myself I'm a little concerned about the expense of someone coming in, because they charge a lot today, and we don't have a lot of extra money to put in to something like that.

W: I know, it is a big concern.

H: And also, I'm concerned about a stranger coming in, not that I distrust everybody, but I do feel distrustful about the possibility of someone taking something, but I guess I'll just feel that way too.

W: But, what are our options if we don't?

H: The only option we have is to continue along as we are, which isn't good because it makes you unhappy; it doesn't bother me too much, as you know.

W: Well, it's embarrassing to me, it's embarrassing to me when anybody comes in and, uh, because it's a reflection on the woman . . . the house, just as the lawn is a reflection on the man if he's able to do it. And now since my cancer was diagnosed, and all the surgeries, and the therapy, it amounts to something that's overwhelming.

H: Due to this cancer situation it's worse than ever.

W: Yeah, it's overwhelming.

H: But, uh, I'm doing the best I can.

W: I know, I know, and I feel guilty even bringing this up, but we need to really pursue this and not get sidetracked. I keep thinking, oh well, another week and I'll be able to do more, and then another treatment and you're not able to do more . . . every few weeks. It's just that it's kinda gotten out of hand. And it does bother me.

H: I know it bothers you.

W: It stresses me. And that makes stress in my life that I could eliminate if I would just get, um . . .

H: Well, I don't want you to have that stress, and maybe we should more seriously consider having someone come in to alleviate you of that stress, especially in view of what you're going through. Because, after all, you're not able to do all the things you used to do around the house. You used to do all those things that I dislike doing—dusting, vacuuming, mopping, this, that, and the other.

After the segment is completed, ask group members if anyone can identify the type of communication portrayed. Supplement the group conversation with the following summary.

Summary

In this example the wife states what she sees as the problem and her feelings about it. She raises the issue in a way that is not nagging or complaining, and expresses appreciation for what her husband has been doing to help. The husband then reflects what he hears his wife defining as the problem before continuing. Both partners express their own feelings while validating those of their partner. They each respect the right of the other to finish speaking and don't interrupt each other. Both accept their own responsibility for the problem and/or the solution and keep the discussion open and moving toward a solution. Both are taking the other's needs into consideration when talking about the problem and the solution, and the husband expresses empathy toward his wife.

Case Vignette 3

The next two vignettes involve a wife expressing her feelings about the physical changes resulting from cancer treatment.

W: You know, when I first became ill and I found out all of this and it happened that my life had changed forever. And the way it had changed is the little things. On the outskirts of it, if someone were to look at it, they would say, "Oh, well that's nothing, that's not important." But to me it is. I think you remember when we first started talking about going through chemotherapy, and I think out of all of the treatments I received, it was the one I was most concerned about, only because of all I've read indicating it was devastating to my body, and my hair was going to fall out, and it could also have other side effects. And I was feeling sad about it. I don't know if I was depressed, but I was feeling sad about looking different. Also not knowing what to expect—the fear of what it would do to my body—how it would change my body and just those kinds of feelings about, especially about how I would look, my appearance, maybe people finding out because I don't have any hair, or because of the way I would look—knowing that I may be sick, that was a big deal to me, and I know for you, or at least I believe for you it was just "one more phase of the treatment," "lets get it done"—that other stuff is just kind of on the periphery . . . .

H: I know you've felt anxieties about the effect that chemotherapy would have on you, but anxiety is an emotion that can cause inaction, and inaction can lead quickly to a bad outcome. When you're in the midst of the battle, that's not the time to be in the process of emotion. I too have had concerns about chemotherapy, but mine have really been primarily, A. would it give us an assurance, or at least as good an assurance as one can be given, that the cancer would not return, and B. what harm would it do in that process? From my perspective, changes in your appearance haven't concerned me, because our relationship, I think, is deeper and more important than appearances—and, um, I don't particularly concern myself with what other people think about any aspect of my life—so cancer isn't any different, so, again, my primary concern has been, was it necessary to effect the outcome that we need and what harm could it potentially do? That's how I've approached this. You have to prioritize, you cannot allow yourself to engage in inaction, when immediate aggressive action is needed. That's just the way I approach things.

After the segment is completed, ask group members if anyone can identify the type of communication portrayed. Supplement the group conversation with the following summary.

Summary

In this segment, the wife begins by talking about her feelings and the effects of the diagnosis and treatment. She tries to express that her husband seems to have minimized the physical and emotional effects of the treatment on her. She brings this up, however, by engaging in negative mind reading. It may have been more effective communication had she used an X-Y-Z statement to express how her husband's behavior/attitude had affected her and made her feel. The husband interrupts his wife and is critical of her expression of emotion. He states his views without reflecting or validating what his wife has expressed. He states that changes in her appearance don't concern him but does not express any understanding that they concern her.

Case Vignette 4

In this final example, a couple is talking about the wife's concern about physical changes due to the cancer treatment.

W: Well. I lost my hair, which I'm actually getting more comfortable with now that it's starting to grow back, and I have what I consider to be very large scars in an area of my breast, um, and one of the biggest problems that I've had—I know we've talked about this before—is the desensitization that you get from people handling an intimate part of your body like they're touching your foot, and adjusting it, and moving it, and putting tattoos on it, and everybody wanting to feel it—{reaching over and touching her husbands imaginary breast} "How is it today? That's good." And pretty much everyone in a lab coat that walks up to you, well, walks up to me, you take your shirt off for. "Hey! Are you here to check this out too?!?" So, then, any time that I've been home and felt like I wanted to be intimate, I felt like I didn't have that intimacy, you know, because it was public domain, and, ah, it's been hard for me to feel relaxed, because sometimes I feel like I'm always just being examined, so I've been having a hard time, since this has all happened because I haven't, uh. I guess essentially I haven't wanted you to touch me because everybody else has been touching me, and anytime that anyone's been touching me, it's been like, you know, finding something wrong, or doing something else, another test, or another injection or another medication. I've been feeling anxiety and depression about this since it's happened and that I won't ever feel like I did before, like I just won't feel sexually attractive, or I just won't feel desirable. And I know that you have said to me that that's not how you look at it, but it's how I feel about it . . .

H: I know . . .

W: like I just won't ever feel like I want to be touched.

H: The scars are there, and I appreciate them, and to me it means this is one more thing that we're going through together. And I don't attribute any baggage to it the same way you do. For me it's a different thing because I don't find you less attractive; this hasn't changed my perception of you as my wife. It doesn't change how I feel about you; it didn't change the way I feel, wanting to hold you and kiss you and touch you.

W: I appreciate you going through this with me, but at the same time, you can only hold my hand up to so far, and then I have to walk through it by myself.

H: I can't change the way you feel about it because it's how you feel about yourself. It has to be something that you're going to have to go through and feel more comfortable with your body at your own speed. All I can do is treat you as I normally would. Does it change how I feel about you? No, it doesn't. The fact that you have no hair? I know you had longer hair, and you've always had long hair, it was a big adjustment for you and you hated it. I know you hated it. But, it doesn't change how I feel about you. You're not a new person, you just have new hair. And, it just looks like a nice short hairstyle. You look good with a buzz cut.

After the segment is completed, ask group members if anyone can identify the type of communication portrayed. Supplement the group conversation with the following summary.

Summary

In this example, the wife expresses very intimate feelings about changes to her physical appearance and sense of intimacy. The husband allows her to complete her thoughts and validates her feelings. The wife expresses appreciation toward her husband. The husband expresses honest feelings that are positive toward his wife, and he states what he feels he *can* do to help deal with the issue. He offers her reassurance and emotional support without minimizing her feelings or changing the focus of the conversation.

Speaker/Listener Technique (30 minutes)

In the next portion of the session instruct the group in the use of the Speaker/Listener Technique. If you have a coleader, have him or her assist in the explanation and demonstration of the technique to the group.

> *Today we have discussed many ways of communicating—some more effective and some less effective. In the first session, you participated in a group discussion on the impact of cancer on your marriages, and we practiced taking turns speaking and listening. The patients had an opportunity to share their thoughts and feelings as a group while the partners listened to their discussions. Then the partners had a chance to review the main issues that they observed. Although this kind of discussion format may not resemble your day-to-day communication style, in fact, this approach may be very helpful to some couples in certain situations.*

Explain the Speaker/Listener Technique as a powerful way to communicate safely and with respect when dealing with tough topics. Let the group know that this communication approach has been widely used by counselors who work with improving interpersonal relationships and is very helpful if couples are willing to try it, practice it, and give it a chance to work. Remind couples that this is not a technique that should necessarily be used all the time. It is a way to communicate safely and clearly when you are dealing with a difficult topic.

Let the group know of the following benefits of the Speaker/Listener Technique:

- A structured discussion makes it hard for feelings to get out of control

- Helps each partner to feel heard

- Minimizes the likelihood of avoiding important issues

- Helps keep communication clear

Review with the group the general guidelines of the technique for both the speaker and the listener. You may wish to write them on the flipchart as group members follow along using the guidelines in the workbook.

General Guidelines for Both the Speaker and the Listener

The speaker is the one with the floor.

The speaker keeps the floor while the listener paraphrases, and until he or she is ready to give up the floor.

You share the floor over the course of a conversation.

One has to start and may say a number of things, and then the floor is passed over to the listener, who becomes the speaker. You switch back and forth.

No trying to solve the problem.

You are focusing on having a discussion that will clarify each partner's thoughts and feelings.

Stay on one subject at a time.

Some subjects are pretty big and can cover a lot of ground. Just be careful not to be talking about many things at once.

You can stop the flow for a moment if something is unclear or not going right.

However, do not stop and get into a big discussion about what each other is not doing right. Just get back on task and follow the suggested guidelines.

Use the "Stop Action."

Choose any signal you both agree on to stop things if you feel things are getting out of hand.

Guidelines for the Speaker

Don't go on and on.

The speaker talks about his or her feelings and concerns in small enough bits that the Listener can paraphrase. You will have plenty of opportunity to say all you want.

After saying a bit, stop and allow the listener to paraphrase what has been said.

If the paraphrase was not quite accurate, the speaker should politely restate the part that was not correctly understood. This is not a test—the goal is to help the listener understand everything the speaker said. Help each other out.

Speak for yourself.

The speaker tries to use "I" statements, talking about their feelings and concerns. "I think you . . . " is not an "I" statement.

You can pass the floor at any time to the listener to hear their side of the issue.

The speaker can ask for feedback, or the listener can ask to comment.

Paraphrase what the speaker is saying.

Briefly repeat what you heard the speaker say, using your own words if you like, and make sure you understood what the speaker meant to convey. Try to include only what you have heard just then, not information about other conversations or your own thoughts.

You can ask for examples or explanations of something the speaker said.

These questions can only be about something the speaker has already said that you are unsure of, not questions challenging them or getting them off track.

Do not offer your opinion or thoughts until you get the floor.

This is the hardest part of being a good listener. Your task is to respond only in the service of understanding the speaker. Any words or gestures to show your opinion are not allowed, including making faces! You will get your turn to speak your mind.

Concentrate on what the speaker is saying, and attempt to edit out your internal responses.

In arguments, people are usually not listening but instead are preparing their next point. Focus on your partner's point of view! Validate your partner by letting them know you understand what they're saying, whether or not you agree.

If you wish, you may briefly demonstrate the Speaker/Listener Technique using a relatively benign topic in order to clarify the exercise for participants. Then, invite participants to try the Speaker/Listener Technique themselves. Instruct couples to choose an issue to discuss. Caution them not to choose a major marital issue or an issue that they frequently argue about. The goal is not to resolve the issue but rather to practice taking turns speaking and listening. Couples should use the Common Courtesies for Effective Communication in the workbook as they practice.

Give couples 10 minutes to practice the Speaker/Listener Technique as you and your coleader walk around the room and observe everyone. If you wish, pass out a visual aid to each couple that represents "the floor." This can be a large piece of construction paper or posterboard with the word "floor" written on it. Couples can use this to keep track of who has "the floor" (i.e., who is speaking). After 10 minutes, reconvene the group and introduce today's homework assignment. Tell couples that they should use the Speaker/Listener Technique to discuss a specific problem they are experiencing related to cancer treatment (either ongoing or completed).

Examples of possible topics include feeling tired or weak from treatment, pain, fears, or worries that they might have, changes in child care or household responsibilities as a result of the illness or treatment, and so forth. Couples may also practice the Speaker/Listener Technique during the week with any topic of their choice. Instruct couples to track their progress using the Instructions for Speaker/Listener Home Assignment in the workbook. Let them know that you will be going over how they liked using the technique at the next meeting.

Guided Imagery Relaxation Exercise (10 minutes)

Next, conduct a Guided Imagery Relaxation exercise. This exercise will guide participants in bringing to mind relaxing images and calming sensory experiences.

Guided Imagery Relaxation Script

The script for the guided imagery is as follows:

Begin by finding a comfortable position and letting your eyes focus on one point in the room. Gradually, allow your eyelids to drift shut. Calmly, I wonder if you can allow your mind to travel . . . to travel far away to a special place, a special place that you would like to share with your partner. Perhaps a place you've enjoyed in the past or a place you've dreamed of experiencing. Someplace calm and peaceful, where you feel comfortable and safe.

Gradually you can begin to see your special place. What is the light like in this place? Perhaps it is soft or bright. You notice that with your thoughts you can control the light in this place, and you turn it up or down just as you want it.

Notice how vibrant the colors are around you, how deep and rich all the shades around you are. And I wonder if you can find how nice it is to adjust those colors and shades with your mind.

What sounds do you hear in your special place? Perhaps it is very still and quiet in this place and you notice what that sounds like too.

What does the air around you feel like? It may be warm and soothing, cool and refreshing. You notice that the air feels just right on your skin and that your skin can begin to tingle with the energy of the air around you. It makes you feel light and refreshed.

And you can begin to become aware of the smells in this special place as you take in the fragrance of the air. It is so comforting.

You may even be able to taste the air as you inhale. You are free to enjoy the soothing sensation of the air with each breath.

And you feel the air cleansing you as it travels into your body through your nose, into your throat, filling your lungs, collecting whatever tension may be in your body. Collecting any tension or uneasiness and taking it away as the air travels back through your body. Taking all troubles away as the air exits your body. All worries and concerns flow right out of you as you exhale. They're not important to you now. You don't need them right now. What's important is that your whole body, from the tip of your toes all the way up to the top of your head, is becoming more and more relaxed and calm in this very safe and private place that belongs solely to you and your partner.

You feel very safe and connected as you and your partner begin to further explore this special place together. Perhaps you are walking hand in hand, your fingertips touching gently, or maybe arm in arm, supporting each other as you move forward together. You feel very secure as you move, noticing how easily and steadily the two of you move together along the surface, and how perfectly comfortable the texture of this surface feels. It may feel very solid beneath you, or soft, or perhaps it is as if you are just floating along. Your whole body just begins to unwind and settle deeper and deeper into a feeling of peaceful calm, as you become more and more relaxed with your partner next to you.

You are alone together and in comfortable control. Maybe one of you is the gentle leader, or perhaps you take turns in leading the discovery in this special place. You delight in the opportunity to share this special place with your partner and relish in their excitement and joy. Though you may have traveled here in the past, you marvel at the new things that you have never noticed before, how this place seems brand new, yet comforting and familiar at the same time.

You feel exhilarated and free in this special place. You delight in knowing that you can stay here for as long as you need. Continuing to take in the sights, . . . sounds, . . . smells, . . . tastes, . . . textures, and feelings of this special place with your partner for as long as you like. You are alone together and in comfortable control.

And perhaps as you experience this place with your partner, the two of you come upon something very special. A magnificent discovery for the two of you to share. A beautiful discovery that fills each of you with peaceful joy. And the two of you quietly pause, savoring and sharing this special treasure, allowing its simple splendor to flow through all of your senses. Feeling every part of your being filled with calm energy as you take in this special treasure that is yours and yours alone, together.

And gently, as you are ready, you share a special sign with your partner that signals it is time to leave this place for now. And so you both allow the treasure that you have discovered together to rest here in this special place. Knowing that it will remain here safe and secure, but that you will hold it and cherish it within your memory until you next return to rediscover it together.

And as you begin to gather yourself to leave this special place, you are comforted by the knowledge that you can return at any time you wish. You know that this is a wonderful way to care for yourself.

And as you are ready, slowly readjust yourself to the sound of my voice. I am going to count slowly backward from 10, and with each count backward, you can become more and more familiar with where you are right now. 10, 9 . . . become aware of the sounds around you . . . 8, 7 . . . become aware of the temperature of the room—how does it feel? How does your body feel? . . . 6, 5 . . . begin to open your eyes now and gradually readjust them to the light around you . . . 4, 3 . . . notice the sense of calm that you have achieved remains with you as you slowly reorient yourself to this room and this place . . .

and . . . notice how good it is to reconnect with everything around you, carrying with you a pleasant feeling of energy for the rest of the day.

Homework (5 minutes)

 ✎ Remind couples to practice using the Speaker/Listener Technique over the course of the next week to discuss a specific problem they are experiencing related to cancer treatment. Check to see if members have any remaining questions about the technique or if they need further clarification.

✎ Instruct group members to use the script in the workbook to practice the guided imagery technique over the course of the next week.

Chapter 7 | *Session 5*

(Corresponds to chapter 5 of the workbook)

Materials Needed

- Flipchart and markers
- Name tags
- Pens/pencils and paper
- Visual aid representing "the floor" (See Chapter 6)

Session Outline

- Review homework (15 minutes)
- Review communication/support material, eliciting group discussion. (20 minutes)
- Have group members practice expressing and listening to support needs with their partners (15 minutes)
- Discuss support needs as a group and share reactions to partner's needs (15 minutes)
- Introduce Caring Days exercise (5 minutes)
- Have couples generate (5 minutes) and discuss (10 minutes) Caring Days wish lists
- Assign homework (5 minutes)

Session Objectives

- To enhance the communication of feelings and support needs between partners

- To enhance the provision of support as a means of caring for one's partner

Homework Review (15 minutes)

To open the group, elicit participants' feedback regarding the home assignments. Ask group members about their experiences using the relaxation techniques with questions such as:

- *How did your practice of the Guided Imagery relaxation technique go?*

- *Have you found any one of the three techniques we have covered to be most effective for you?*

- *Are there situations in which you have used or anticipate using one of these techniques to help you deal with feelings of stress?*

- *Have there been any situations in which you have been able to encourage your partner in using one of these techniques?*

Next, briefly review the Speaker/Listener Technique and X-Y-Z Technique homework from last week. Elicit general comments about the exercises and check to see if all participants attempted and completed the homework; if they did not, inquire about what barriers prevented them from completing the task. Pose the following questions to the group:

- *Did you or your partner bring up any issues of which you were previously unaware?*

- *How well did you understand your partner's point of view?*

- *Did you feel listened to and understood by your partner?*

- *How was using this technique similar to or different from previous discussions?*

■ *What aspects of the technique are most difficult for you or require more work?*

Communication and Coping (20 minutes)

Next, focus the group on linking communication and coping with cancer.

During the past several weeks we have spoken a lot about communication, in general, and about more and less effective ways of communicating with your partner. Maintaining good communication is important in any relationship, and it's a challenge that a couple deals with on a daily basis. Good communication only becomes more important at times when you are dealing with something like cancer. We've spent some time talking about how effective communication between partners can improve coping and problem-solving abilities. We're going to talk about a related set of issues today. that is, the large role that communication plays in how the two of you provide and receive support during stressful times. Effective communication is essential in expressing our feelings and needs to others and in responding to the feelings and needs of others, as well.

Ask group members for reasons why a person might not disclose his or her feelings or needs. Write responses on the flipchart. Supplement group comments with the following common reasons:

■ Trying to avoid burdening the other with your worries, fears, or requests for assistance

■ Trying to avoid any arguments for fear of upsetting the other

■ Fearful of hurting the other person (don't know how to say it)

■ Don't want to appear needy or show vulnerability

■ Worry that the other might not care or might not respond in the way you'd like

Discuss with the group the possibility that people sometimes do not disclose their feelings or needs to their partners because they are trying not to hurt their partner's feelings or make them worry. Explain that research has found that couples in cancer treatment who tend to conceal their feelings in an effort to protect their partner are less satisfied with their relationships later on and also evidence more distress.

Impart to the group the following reasons why it is important to disclose feelings and needs:

- People do not know what you need/want/feel unless you tell them.

- In disclosing feelings or needs, you may obtain suggestions about ways to cope.

- Not disclosing feelings or needs can block the lines of communication.

- Undisclosed issues may cause resentment or hostile feelings.

- You cause yourself undue stress by keeping negative feelings inside; both physical and emotional health suffers when we are burdened by undisclosed problems.

Ask group members: *"Can anyone suggest what someone who is disclosing a feeling may want from the listener?*

Try to elicit from participants the following responses:

- To feel understood and listened to

- To feel loved and accepted

- To feel that someone empathizes with what they are feeling

- To feel close with the other person

Ask group members: *"Can anyone suggest what someone who is disclosing a feeling may* not *want from the listener?"*

Try to elicit from participants the following responses:

- Solutions offered too fast (a "quick fix" to the problem or issue)

- To feel like the topic was changed, to either another person or another issue

- To feel criticized, rejected, dismissed, or avoided

In order to have interchanges that promote productive disclosure of feelings, couples can use the Speaker/Listener Technique introduced last week. Tell members that if they find themselves as the listener in an unstructured situation (where the Speaker/Listener Technique is not being utilized), he or she should reflect what the speaker is saying, inviting further disclosure. Give the following example:

Speaker: "I feel tired and crabby."

Listener: "It sounds like you're having a bad day . . . "

Explain that sometimes a person needs some encouragement or invitation to begin disclosure. In this case, the listener could initiate a conversation by noting their impression of the other's behavior, which is indicating distress or repressed feelings.

Remind group members that it is important not to push too hard or be demanding or critical when attempting to get another person to disclose his or her feelings. Give the following example of what to say:

"You seem to be sleeping a lot lately/looking sad/drinking more than usual. Is there anything I can do for you, anything you want to talk about?" Or even simply, "How are you feeling?"

Give the following examples of what *not* to say:

"Why don't you ever talk to me? Just tell me what's wrong already . . . "

"You know, you have to start letting your feelings out"

"I don't know why you have such a hard time opening up."

"What's the matter now?"

Continue the discussion by saying:

> It is important to remember that there may be differences in the intentions of the speaker and listener with regard to the purpose of disclosing feelings.
>
> Problems may ensue when the goal of the speaker is to talk about the problem and be understood, while the listener's goal is to come up with a solution for the problem. When what the speaker wants is a good listener, getting advice or solutions to the problem may make the speaker feel distanced, since he or she is not getting the understanding and empathy desired.

Discuss with the group the following ways of avoiding distancing the speaker:

- Do not jump in with advice before the person is ready. Often, people will *ask* for advice when they want it.

- Let the person get all their feelings out . . . be understanding.

- Be a good listener!

    By allowing our partner the opportunity to express his or her feelings and needs, we can be a better "partner" to them. You will be better able to understand how you can best support them.

    Both the patient and the partner need support in dealing with cancer and its treatment.

Discuss with couples the following types of support *patients* may need from their partners:

- Emotional support to help deal with feelings about the illness, fear, worries, treatment, children, the future, physical limitations, side effects, etc.

- Tangible support to help deal with limitations on ability to work, do household chores, take care of the children, etc.

- Self-esteem support to bolster self-esteem and help the patient not feel bad about herself and validating her worth as a person

Discuss with couples the following types of support *partners* may need from the patients:

- Emotional support to help deal with feelings about partner's illness, fear, worries, treatment, children, the future, etc.

- Self-esteem support to bolster self-esteem and validate the partner's worth as a person, a caregiver, and a partner

After this discussion, move on to having members practice using the Speaker/Listener Technique to discuss their individual support needs with their partners. You may use the following sample dialogue to facilitate the exercise:

As we speak about support needs, it's important to point out that each individual's support needs are unique and may vary in different situations. Oftentimes, it is difficult to determine what your own needs are, and even harder to know what your partner needs from you and others. You are now going to have an opportunity to directly communicate your support needs to your partner.

We would now like for each of you to use the Speaker/Listener Technique to discuss your individual support needs with your partner.

Speaker/Listener Technique Practice (15 minutes)

Give the group time to practice using the Speaker/Listener Technique to answer the question, *"What is it that you need from each other as you go through cancer treatment and recovery?"* Instruct each partner of a couple to take turns stating his or her needs while the other partner simply listens. The partner who is listening should restate what he or she has heard. Provide the visual aid depicting "the floor" so couples can keep track of who "holds the floor" (i.e., who is actually speaking). Make sure that each partner has an opportunity to share. Do this for 15 minutes.

Group Discussion (15 minutes)

Then, reconvene the large group and ask each group member to comment on his or her own needs, as well as the needs of his or her partner. You may use the following questions to focus the group discussion:

- *What was it like for you to hear your partner's needs?*

- *Do these needs seem reasonable? Why? Why not?*

- *What are some things that prevent you from fulfilling these needs?*

Encourage group members to respond to one another. The full-group discussion should last for approximately 15 minutes.

Caring Days Exercise (5 minutes)

Introduce the Caring Days exercise as follows:

One of the common barriers to providing our partners with the support they need is not knowing what they want. Sometimes even when needs are communicated, we may still be unclear about how to specifically fulfill that need. For instance, if your partner tells you he or she would like you to be more considerate, does that mean asking your partner how he or she is feeling, buying your partner something special, calling during the day just to say "hi," or something else?

One exercise that has been proven to help couples to meet each other's needs is called Caring Days. To complete Caring Days, each partner separately composes a wish list of at least 10 small things that his or her partner could do for him or her that would bring him or her pleasure.

Ask yourself, "Exactly what would you like your partner to do as a means of showing that he or she cares for you? What would you put on your wish list that your partner could do for you?" For instance, the list might include making or buying coffee one morning for the other partner, serving breakfast in bed, planning a date for the other partner, driving carpool, giving a massage, and so on. Maybe you would like your partner to encourage and assist you in engaging in relaxation by playing with the children so you can relax, or by running a warm bath for you and putting on your favorite music.

The wish list requests that you make of your partner should meet the following criteria:

They must be positive.

They must be specific.

They must be small behaviors that can be done at least once daily.

A positive request aims for an increase in constructive behaviors, not a decrease in unwanted responses. "Please ask me how my arm feels today" is a positive request, whereas "Please do not continue to watch television when I am asking you a question" is a negative request.

A specific request is one that is easily understood, such as, "Watch a movie with me on Friday night," instead of a vague request like, "Act a little more sensitive when I have radiation."

Allow 5 minutes for group members to create individual wish lists.

Next, have partners exchange lists and discuss, with each other, the requests on their respective lists. The partner making the list should state his or her requests as specifically as possible. The partner receiving the list should ask for clarification about any ambiguous requests. Allow 10 minutes for this portion of the session.

Close the session by summarizing today's topics, responding to any questions or concerns, and assigning homework. When assigning the Caring Days exercise, you may wish to use the following sample dialogue:

We would like each of you to try to fulfill some of the items on your partner's wish list during the next week. You may want to try to surprise each other, or you may want to discuss and plan Caring Days activities together. Whichever you prefer is fine. This activity is helpful in making partners' needs known to each other and enhancing that sense of caring within your relationship.

Homework (5 minutes)

 ✎ Instruct group members to fulfill some of the items on their partners' wish list during the next week.

Chapter 8 | *Session 6*

(Corresponds to chapter 6 of the workbook)

Materials Needed

- Flipchart and markers
- Name tags
- Pens/pencils and paper

Session Outline

- Review homework (10 minutes)
- Outline psychosocial challenges of cancer survivorship and expectations for continued recovery (10 minutes)
- Have couples construct Priority Pie Charts for Before and After Cancer (20 minutes)
- Conduct couple-specific discussion of ways of coping with future demands of cancer, leading to the nomination of a "motto" for living with cancer (10 minutes)
- Present pies and mottoes to the rest of the group with interview by group leaders (20 minutes)
- Wrap-up discussion (20 minutes)

Session Objectives

- To help couples achieve insight into the changes that have occurred in their priorities since the diagnosis of cancer

- To assist couples in planning for the survivorship phase

Homework Review (5 minutes)

Begin today's session by welcoming the group to the final meeting. Review the home assignment (Caring Days) and ask participants to share with the group their experiences in completing the activity. You may use the following questions to guide the discussion of the home assignment:

- *What activities did you complete for your partner? What did he or she do for you?*

- *What barriers prevented you from completing these activities?*

- *What did you learn about yourself and your partner from these exercises?*

After reviewing the homework, present the material on cancer survivorship and continued recovery.

Cancer Survivorship and Continued Recovery (20 minutes)

For the past several weeks, the focus of the group has been on the impact of cancer on couples' relationships and daily family life. When couples are in the midst of undergoing active treatment for cancer, it is understandable that much of daily life revolves around the practical and emotional demands of treatment.

Explain to couples that, given the fact that they often schedule their lives according to medical appointments and the associated "good" and "bad" days, it is not surprising that they look forward to completing the "arduous marathon" that is also known as modern-day cancer treatment. After weeks or months of living by the rules of the treatment protocol, there is often much joy, relief, and satisfaction that comes from the freedom of having completed one's treatment. However, what often takes patients and their partners by surprise is that reaching the treatment "finish line" is often fraught with some unanticipated emotions—fear, isolation, confusion, sadness, and difficulty resuming ones' pre-illness roles, responsibilities, and activities.

Continue the discussion by stating the following:

Many patients describe not realizing what they have been through until they complete treatment. It is understandable to expect that one will bounce back quickly once treatment is complete; however, thanks to the outspoken words of the growing legion of breast cancer survivors, we are learning more and more about the long-term physical and psychological recovery process. Post-traumatic stress responses, fatigue, low sexual desire, and fear of recurrence are some of the more common challenges to posttreatment recovery.

It is thought that one factor that affects adjustment to the posttreatment period of breast cancer is the response of others around you. Understandably, you and your "cheering squad" are eager to see you return to your old self. Many cancer survivors, even those who had excellent support during the rigors of active treatment, observe that once treatment is over, their social support network "changes the channel" and infrequently or never brings up the topic of cancer. Not that patients want to be "stuck on the cancer channel," but realistically it is more often the case that cancer-related issues do not spontaneously end when the treatment protocol is finished. Follow-up medical appointments, the anniversary of the cancer diagnosis, treatment-related side effects, new physical symptoms, hearing about a celebrity diagnosed with cancer, and even the "Kleenex Movie of the Week" can evoke vivid memories and fears. Furthermore, individuals, even those within the same family, may have a different speed of recovery from cancer and its treatment. Some folks may be more like the "quick hare," whereas others may more closely resemble the "slow tortoise." Because these differing speeds of recovery can be frustrating for some couples, it remains important to maintain open communication regarding cancer-related issues well after the last chemotherapy or radiation treatment.

Coping with cancer survivorship often involves reevaluating your coping with cancer game plan to be certain that it fits the new challenges of balancing the ongoing demands of cancer with the desire to "move on" and fully resume one's roles and routines. This is where knowing your own and your relationship priorities comes in. Chances are many things have taken a back burner while you've been fighting cancer. Being clear about what really matters to you helps to reestablish priorities, reduce your feeling of being overwhelmed, and work toward restoring a sense of equilibrium between cancer and noncancer priorities.

Priority Pie Chart Activity (20 minutes)

Discuss with the group the fact that cancer inevitably changes couples' priorities. You may use the following sample dialogue to facilitate discussion:

For almost all couples, cancer inevitably changes their priorities. With all the stresses that come with coping with cancer, many couples find that it becomes clear to them what matters most. After confronting cancer, many couples find that things that they may have considered most important prior to the illness are now less important. On the contrary, things that they may not have thought about prior to the cancer diagnosis suddenly take on great importance after cancer centers their lives. Having a clear sense of priorities is helpful and should help guide couples' coping efforts.

We would like for you to sit down with your partner and consider how your priorities as a couple have changed or stayed the same as a result of confronting cancer. We would like you to display your priorities visually.

Refer couples to the Priority Pie Chart pages in the workbook. Explain that one chart will be used to depict each couple's priorities "before cancer," and the other will depict the couple's priorities "after cancer." Be sure to stress to the group that the pie charts should represent the priorities of the *couple* and not the individuals within the couple. Instruct couples to divide each circle in the workbook into slices of pie, with each slice representing one of the couple's priorities. Tell couples to make each slice as big as they feel is appropriate to represent each priority and to make as many slices as they wish. Some examples of pie slices or priorities might include spirituality (attending spiritual services, observing holidays and rituals), family (spending time with kids, time with partner), career, health, money, intimacy, physical exercise, or whatever each couple finds important.

Show the group a model pie chart and walk around the room and respond to any questions that couples might have while completing the activity. Notify couples when there are 5 minutes remaining and encourage couples to complete their pie charts.

Creating a Motto for Living With Cancer (10 minutes)

Introduce couples to the next activity, which includes a couple-specific discussion of ways of coping with future demands of cancer and the creation of a motto for living with cancer.

Ask them to review their completed pie charts and consider those priorities that they want to maintain, reestablish, or develop further in the future. Ask each couple to also think about the changes in their relationship that are depicted in their pie charts and the goals they have for the future based on the priorities they have identified. Couples should use this information to create a motto or theme describing their future relationship in terms of "living with cancer." Mottoes should be true to couples' priorities and should reflect their attitude toward the future, keeping the illness in mind. Mottoes do not need to be fancy; they should just reflect each couple's hopes and desires for how they would like their marriage to look in the future as they leave cancer treatment behind and enter the cancer survivorship phase. Examples of possible mottoes include:

- "Together we stand, divided we fall."

- "Live strong together."

- "Health and family now."

Have group members remain paired off in couples to complete this task. After approximately 10 minutes, reconvene the group and ask the couples to share their pie charts and mottoes with the group.

Group Presentation (20 minutes)

As each couple shares their pies and motto, interview them as the rest of the group observes.

> *Let's say that we visit with you next year, how do you imagine marital life would look? Pay particular attention to what would be the same; what would be more like things used to be; what new things would we see.*

Gradually move into more general discussion about "Our relationship one year from now" and use the following questions to frame discussion:

- *Where do you want to be, and how will you get there?*

- *What barriers do you anticipate might be in your way as you go about trying to reach your goals?*

- *Why are these objectives/goals important for your relationship? How do they fit with your priorities?*

- *Can you say anything about the meaning of this cancer experience to you as a couple?*

After each couple has presented their future goals and motto and received feedback, engage the group in a wrap-up discussion.

Closing the Session (20 minutes)

Review the major concepts of the six sessions, including communication, stress management and relaxation, coping with cancer, thinking about changes in thinking and behaving due to cancer, and learning to talk about feelings. You may want to use the outlines for the six sessions from Chapter 1 and remind couples, *"In the first session we learned about . . . . In the second session . . . "*

Then, ask group members for their thoughts and feelings about the final session. Encourage participation from those members who seem reticent to share their thoughts. For example, you may say something like the following: *"I wonder if anyone else feels similarly to Jim?"* You can encourage quiet members by saying something like, *"Jane, you have been rather quiet. Do you have any thoughts?"*

Ask also for couples' feedback regarding the group, and for suggestions for future groups. You might ask:

- *What did you learn from the group?*

- *What was the most memorable session? The most useful exercise?*

- *What was the least helpful aspect of the group?*

- *What suggestions do you have for improving the group?*

Emphasize that the skills group members have attained through attending sessions require practice, and that couples owe it to themselves to continue rehearsing what they have learned. You may wish to use the following sample dialogue:

> *Attending these sessions has likely been helpful not only because of the skills you may have learned but also because you and your partner have made a commitment to attend these groups together. These hours attending groups and completing home assignments represent time that you have spent alone together, working on your relationship. It is important to continue to make quality time for each other; the past 6 weeks have demonstrated that it is possible to do so. You owe it to yourselves and each other to take what you have learned here and to practice it; practice good communication and relaxation skills, make time for each other, and take care of yourselves and each other. Remember your Intimacy Deck and Caring Days activities. These are tools to use along with the skills you have learned to help you in your day-to-day relationship.*

Ask if there are any final questions or concerns. Provide group members with a telephone number that they may use in order to receive a referral for ongoing counseling. You may also wish to provide them with the Blueprint for Cancer Survivors and Their Loved Ones (see Appendix A). Be sure to use the space provided to fill in contact information for local cancer support resources in your community. You may photocopy the appendix and distribute as necessary. Then, thank members for their participation and dismiss the group.

Community Resources

List local breast cancer resources (e.g., organizations, support groups, medical providers) in the space provided.

_____

_____

_____

_____

_____

_____

Y-ME National Support Hotline

Speak with a breast cancer survivor; obtain information, support, referrals.

1-800-221-2141

National Cancer Institute's Cancer Information Service

A free, national information and education network organized by the nation's primary agency for cancer research. Offers the latest, most accurate cancer information through a confidential program, in both English and Spanish.

1-800-4-CANCER

Gilda's Club

Named in honor of Gilda Radner. A place where people with cancer and their families and friends join with others to build social and emotional support. Offers support and networking groups, lectures, workshops, and social events in a homelike setting. All activities are free of charge.

1-212-647-9700

Cancer Care

Offers counseling and emotional support via professional oncology social workers, professionally led support groups, educational seminars, teleconferences, treatment information, and referrals. All services are provided free of charge and are available to people of all ages.

1-800-813-HOPE (4673)

(see section on Online Resources for URL)

Look Good Feel Better

Licensed cosmetologists teach women undergoing cancer treatment how to enhance their appearance by using accessories and makeup techniques.

1-800-395-LOOK

American Cancer Society

Cancer information and referrals.

1-800-ACS-2345

Online Resources

National Alliance of Breast Cancer Organizations

Offers news updates, bulletins, breast cancer facts, support groups, information on workshops conferences.

www.nabco.org

American Cancer Society

www.cancer.org

Cancer Information Service (NCI)

www.cis.nci.nih.gov

CancerNet

Cancer information compiled by the National Cancer Institute and National Institutes of Health.

www.cancernet.nci.nhi.gov

NCI Office of Cancer Survivorship

Learn what's new in cancer survivorship and about the ongoing research on survivorship supported by the National Cancer Institute.

www.dcps.nci.nih.gov/OCS/

Y-ME National Breast Cancer Organization

Offers information about breast cancer, Y-Me services, support groups, links to other sites.

www.y-me.org

Breast Cancer Online

Offering breast cancer news groups that allow you to share information with others, e-mail subscriptions, a resources page, listings of organizations to aid in all phases of cancer care.

www.breastcanceronline.com

America Online

Keyword: Avon (for a bulletin board dedicated solely to breast cancer support and information). Also look at America Online's Health and Medical Forum. Users of e-mail can subscribe to a breast cancer electronic mailing list. Breast cancer patients and their families, friends, and health professionals share information and support through e-mail messages. To subscribe send e-mail to LISTSERV@morgan.ucs.mun.ca and write SUBSCRIBE BREAST-CANCER in the text of the message.

Men Against Breast Cancer

A nonprofit organization designed to provide targeted support services to educate and empower men to be effective caregivers when cancer strikes a female loved one.

www.menagainstbreastcancer.org

Appendix B *Fidelity Checklists*

SESSION 1
Fidelity Checklist

Date: _____   TAPE #: _____

Therapists: _____

Group: _____

Rate your fidelity to each session element on a scale of 1 to 7, with 1 indicating poor fidelity and 7 indicating high fidelity.

	Actual
Rating:	**Time:**

_____ Introduce yourself and your coleader and describe format of the first session (5 minutes)   _____

_____ Provide overview of the program (5 minutes)   _____

_____ Conduct icebreaker: getting to know you exercise (20 minutes)   _____

_____ Have one group leader meet with small subgroup of patients to discuss patient perspective on cancer and its effect on marital life while partners observe (15 minutes)   _____

_____ Partners, led by group coleader, reflect on patient subgroup discussion (10 minutes)   _____

_____ Have one group leader meet with small subgroup of partners to discuss the partner perspective on cancer and its effect on marital life while patients observe (15 minutes)   _____

_____ Patients, led by group coleader, reflect on partner subgroup discussion (10 minutes)   _____

_____ Review schedule of meetings and administrative information (5 minutes) _____

Notes:

SESSION 2
Fidelity Checklist

Date: _____   TAPE #: _____

Therapists: _____

Group: _____

Rate your fidelity to each session element on a scale of 1 to 7, with 1 indicating poor fidelity and 7 indicating high fidelity.

	Actual
Rating:	**Time:**

_____Review previous session (10 minutes)   _____

_____Present material on cancer-related stress (30 minutes)   _____

_____Conduct the Reading the Signs of Stress exercise and have couples participate
in the "Not-So-Newlywed Game" (30 minutes)   _____

_____Introduce relaxation techniques and lead group in Focused Breathing
exercise (15 minutes)   _____

_____Assign homework (5 minutes)   _____

Notes:

SESSION 3
Fidelity Checklist

Date: _____   TAPE #: _____

Therapists: _____

Group: _____

Rate your fidelity to each session element on a scale of 1 to 7, with 1 indicating poor fidelity and 7 indicating high fidelity.

Rating:		Actual Time:
_____	Review homework (10 minutes)	_____
_____	Introduce coping with stress material (10 minutes)	_____
_____	Introduce material on physical affection and sexuality (10 minutes)	_____
_____	Present sex and cancer case vignette and discuss group reactions (25 minutes)	_____
_____	Have couples create an Intimacy Deck in session (15 minutes)	_____
_____	Describe Sensate Focus (5 minutes)	_____
_____	Conduct Progressive Muscle Relaxation exercise in group (10 minutes)	_____
_____	Assign homework (5 minutes)	_____

Notes:

SESSION 4
Fidelity Checklist

Date: _____   TAPE #: _____

Therapists: _____

Group: _____

Rate your fidelity to each session element on a scale of 1 to 7, with 1 indicating poor fidelity and 7 indicating high fidelity.

		Actual
Rating:		**Time:**
_____	Review homework (10 minutes)	_____
_____	Lead interactive discussion on communication, making sure to talk about the differences between good and bad communication (15 minutes)	_____
_____	Review case vignettes depicting conversations between breast cancer patients and their spouses (20 minutes)	_____
_____	Introduce Speaker/Listener Technique and have couples practice the technique (30 minutes)	_____
_____	Conduct Guided Imagery Relaxation exercise (10 minutes)	_____
_____	Assign homework (5 minutes)	_____

Notes:

SESSION 5
Fidelity Checklist

Date: _____   TAPE #: _____

Therapists: _____

Group: _____

Rate your fidelity to each session element on a scale of 1 to 7, with 1 indicating poor fidelity and 7 indicating high fidelity.

Rating:

                                                                    **Actual
                                                                    Time:**

_____ Review homework (15 minutes)   _____

_____ Review communication/support material, eliciting group discussion
(20 minutes)   _____

_____ Have group members practice expressing and listening to support needs
with their partners (15 minutes)   _____

_____ Discuss support needs as a group and share reactions to partner's needs
(15 minutes)   _____

_____ Introduce Caring Days exercise (5 minutes)   _____

_____ Have couples generate (5 minutes) and discuss (10 minutes) Caring Days
wish lists   _____

_____ Assign homework (5 minutes)   _____

Notes:

SESSION 6
Fidelity Checklist

Date: _____   TAPE #: _____

Therapists: _____

Group: _____

Rate your fidelity to each session element on a scale of 1 to 7, with 1 indicating poor fidelity and 7 indicating high fidelity.

Rating: **Actual Time:**

_____Review homework (10 minutes)   _____

_____Outline psychosocial challenges of cancer survivorship and expectations for continued recovery (10 minutes)   _____

_____Have couples construct Priority Pie Charts for Before and After Cancer (20 minutes)   _____

_____Conduct couple-specific discussion of ways of coping with future demands of cancer, leading to the nomination of a "motto" for living with cancer (10 minutes)   _____

_____Present pies and mottoes to the rest of the group, with interview by group leaders (20 minutes)   _____

_____Wrap-up discussion (20 minutes)   _____

Notes:

References

Beck, A., Rush, A., Shaw, B., & Emery, G. (1979). *Cognitive Therapy of Depression*. Guilford Press.

Benson, H. (1975). *The relaxation response*. New York, Morrow.

Burish, T., Snyder, S L., Jenkins, R. (1991). Preparing patients for cancer chemotherapy: The effect of coping preparation and relaxation therapies. *Journal of Consulting and Clinical Psychology, 59*, 518–525.

Carver, C. S., Pozo, C., Harris, S., Noriega, V., Scheier, M., Robinson, D., Ketcham, A., Moffat, F., & Clark, K. (1993). How coping mediates the effect of optimism on distress: A study of women with early stage breast cancer. *Journal of Personality and Social Psychology, 65*, 375–390.

Davis, M., Robbins Eshelman, E., McKay, M. (1982). The relaxation and stress reduction handbook. New Harbinger Publications, Oakland, CA.

Gonzales, S., Steinglass, P., & Reiss, D. (1989). Putting the illness in its lace: Discussion groups for families with chronic medical illnesses. Family Process, 28, 69–87.

Gottman, J., Notarius, C., Gonso, J., & Markman, H. (1976). *A couples guide to communication*. Champaign, IL: Research Press.

Jacobson, E. (1974). *Progressive Relaxation*. Chicago: The University of Chicago Press, Midway Reprint.

Kalaitzi, C., Papadopoulos, V., Michas, K. Vlasis, K., Skandalakis, P., & Filippou, D. (2007). *Combined brief psychosexual intervention after mastectomy: Effects on sexuality, body image, and psychological well-being, 96*, 235–240.

Kaplan, H. (1974). *The New Sex Therapy*. New York, Brunner/Mazel.

Lazarus, R., & Folkman, S. (1984). Stress, appraisal and coping. New York: Springer Publications.

Loscalzo, M., & Jacobsen, P. B. (1990). Practical behavioral approaches to effective management of pain and distress. *Journal of Psychosocial Oncology, 8*, 136–139.

Manne, S., Dougherty, J., Veach, S., & Kless, R. (1999). Hiding worries from one's spouse: Protective buffering among Cancer patients and their spouses. *Cancer Research, Therapy and Control, 8,* 175–188.

Manne, S., Norton, T., Ostroff, J., Winkel, G., Fox, K., & Grana, G. (2007). Protective buffering and psychological distress among couples coping with breast cancer: The moderating role of relationship satisfaction. *Journal of Family Psychology,* 21(3), 380–388.

Manne, S., & Ostroff, J. (unpublished data). Couple-focused group intervention for women with early stage breast cancer and their partners: A Pilot Study.

Manne, S., Taylor, K., Dougherty, J., & Kemeny, N. (1997). Supportive and negative responses in the partner relationship: Their association with psychological adjustment among individuals with cancer. *Journal of Behavioral Medicine, 20(2),* 101–125.

Manne, S., Ostroff, J., Norton, T., Fox, K., Goldstein, L., & Grana, G. (2006). Cancer-Related Relationship Communication in Couples Coping with Early Stage Breast Cancer. *Psycho-Oncology, 15,* 234–247.

Manne, S., Ostroff, J., Sherman, M., Heyman, R., & Ross, S., & Fox, K. (2004). Couples' support-related communication, psychological distress, and relationship satisfaction among women with early stage breast cancer. *Journal of Consulting and Clinical Psychology, 72(4),* 660–670.

Manne, S., Ostroff, J., Winkel, G., Goldstein, L., Fox, K., & Grana, G. (2004). Posttraumatic growth following breast cancer: Patient, partner and couple perspectives. *Psychosomatic Medicine, 66,* 442–452.

Manne, S., Ostroff, J., Winkel, G., Fox, K., Grana, G., Miller, E., & Frazier, T. (2005). Couple-Focused Group Intervention for Women with Early Stage Breast Cancer. *Journal of Consulting and Clinical Psychology, 73(4),* 634–646.

Manne, S., Ostroff, J., & Winkel, G. (in press). Social-Cognitive Processes as Moderators of a Couple-Focused Group Intervention for Women with Early Stage Breast Cancer. *Health Psychology.*

Manne, S., Ostroff, J., Winkel, G., Grana, G., & Fox, K. (2005). Partner Unsupportive Responses, Avoidance and Distress among Women with Early Stage Breast Cancer: Patient and Partner Perspectives. *Health Psychology,* 24(6), 635–641.

Manne, S., Pape, S., Taylor, K., & Dougherty, J. (1999). Spouse support, coping, and mood among individuals with cancer. *Annals of Behavioral Medicine,* 21(2), 111–121.

Markman, H. & Floyd, F. (1980). Possibilities for the prevention of marital discord: A behavioral perspective. *American Journal of Family Therapy*, 8, 29–48.

Masters, W., & Johnson, V. (1966). *Human Sexual Response*. Boston: Little, Brown.

Nezu, A., Nezu, C., Felgoise, S., McClure, K. & Houts, P. (2003). Project Genesis: Assessing the Efficacy of problem-solving therapy for distressed adult cancer patients. *Journal of Consulting and Clinical Psychology*, 71, 1036–1048.

Northouse, L., Templin, T., & Mood, D. (2001) Couples' adjustment to breast disease during the first year following diagnosis. *Journal of Behavioral Medicine*, 24, 115–136.

Ostroff, J., Steinglass, P., Ross, S., Ronis-Tobin, V., & Singh, B. (2004). Interest in and barriers to participation in multiple family discussion groups among head and neck cancer survivors and their primary family caregivers. *Family Process*, 43, 195–208.

Pistrang, N. & Barker, C. (1992). Disclosure of concerns in breast cancer. *Psycho-Oncology*, 1, 183–192.

Pistrang, N., & Barker, C. (1995). The partner relationship in psychological response to breast cancer. *Social Science and Medicine, 40,* 789–797.

Scott, J., Halford, W., & Ward, B. (2004). United We Stand? The effects of a couple-coping intervention on adjustment to early stage breast or gynecological cancer. *Journal of Consulting and Clinical Psychology*, 72, 1122–1135.

About the Authors

Sharon L. Manne received her PhD in Clinical Psychology from Arizona State University in 1987. She is currently a Senior Member in the Population Science Division at the Fox Chase Cancer Center in Philadelphia, as well as Adjunct Professor in the College of Health Professions at Temple University and Adjunct Professor in the Oncological Sciences Program at Mount Sinai School of Medicine in New York. Dr. Manne is a recognized international expert in relationship processes in couples coping with cancer, as well as the development and testing of couple-focused psychological interventions for women diagnosed with early stage breast cancer and their partners. Dr. Manne has been elected to Fellow status in the Health Psychology Division and the Pediatric Psychology Division of the American Psychological Association and to Fellow status in the Society of Behavioral Medicine. She has published more than 100 journal articles and book chapters on these and related topics. Dr. Manne's research has been continuously funded since 1990 by grants from the National Institutes of Health, the Department of Defense, and the American Cancer Society.

Jamie S. Ostroff received a PhD in Clinical Psychology from Vanderbilt University in 1988. She is currently an Associate Member and Chief, Behavioral Sciences Service, in the Department of Psychiatry and Behavioral Sciences at Memorial Sloan-Kettering Cancer Center. Dr. Ostroff is a recognized expert in the psychological and behavioral issues in cancer prevention, early detection, treatment, and long-term survivorship. She has published more than 80 journal articles and book chapters on these and related topics. Dr. Ostroff's research has been funded by grants from the National Institutes of Health, the American Cancer Society, the Lance Armstrong Foundation, and the Robert Wood Johnson Foundation.